SAM ALTMAN BIOGRAPHY

FROM STARTUP SUCCESS TO LEADING A TECH REVOLUTION"

ANDERSON C. SMITH

TABLE OF CONTENT

INTRODUCTION

The Visionary Who's Shaping the Future

In the ever-evolving world of technology and innovation, some figures stand out not just for their accomplishments, but for the transformative impact they have on entire industries. Sam Altman is one such individual—a visionary whose relentless drive and keen insights have propelled him to the forefront of the tech world. From his early days as a startup founder to becoming a leading figure in artificial intelligence and tech entrepreneurship, Altman's career has been marked by a deep understanding of technological trends, a willingness to challenge conventional wisdom, and a desire to shape the future for the better.

A Unique Blend of Talent and Timing

Altman's journey began with a combination of talent, timing, and a penchant for thinking ahead of the curve. Born in 1985 in St. Louis, Missouri, he demonstrated an early interest in computers and technology. He learned to program at a young age, which not only gave him a technical foundation but also sparked his curiosity about what technology could do to improve lives. Unlike many others who see technology as a career path, for Altman, it was a tool for reshaping the world, solving significant problems, and creating opportunities for future generations.

Altman's entry into the world of startups came while he was still a student at Stanford University. In 2005, he co-founded Loopt, a location-based social networking app that predated the location-aware services we now take for granted. Although Loopt did not achieve massive commercial success, it taught Altman invaluable lessons about product development, market fit, and the dynamics of the startup ecosystem. His journey with Loopt ended with a sale to Green Dot Corporation in 2012, but the experience solidified his reputation as a young entrepreneur to watch.

Scaling Impact Through Y Combinator

The pivotal moment in Altman's career came when he joined Y Combinator (YC), a highly influential startup accelerator that has helped launch some of the most successful companies in Silicon Valley, including Airbnb, Dropbox, and Reddit. When Paul Graham, one of YC's founders, invited Altman to become a partner in

2011, it marked the beginning of a new chapter in his life—one where he would not only build companies but also help others bring their entrepreneurial visions to life.

As president, and later chairman, of Y Combinator, Altman brought a bold vision for the future. He saw YC not merely as an incubator but as a platform to transform the startup industry. He expanded the number of companies YC funded each year and broadened its reach globally, making it more accessible to entrepreneurs outside of Silicon Valley. Under his leadership, YC invested in startups that tackled diverse challenges, from biotech and artificial intelligence to clean energy and social impact. Altman's ability to identify promising founders and disruptive ideas became a driving force behind YC's continued success, solidifying its reputation as a breeding ground for innovation.

The OpenAI Chapter: Balancing Ethics and Ambition

While Y Combinator allowed Altman to scale his impact by supporting thousands of startups, his next move was even more ambitious. In 2015, he co-founded OpenAI with a mission to ensure that artificial intelligence (AI) benefits all of humanity. The idea was to advance AI in a responsible way, balancing the pursuit of cutting-edge technology with a commitment to safety, ethics, and accessibility. Unlike many AI ventures that focus solely on commercial applications, OpenAI was founded as a non-profit research organization, putting societal benefit at the forefront.

Altman's work at OpenAI has placed him at the center of the ongoing debate about the future of AI. As the technology has advanced rapidly, so have concerns about its ethical implications, including potential job displacement, privacy issues, and even existential risks to humanity. Altman has taken a proactive approach, advocating for policies that prioritize safety and ethical considerations, while still pushing the boundaries of what AI can achieve. His leadership at OpenAI represents a dual ambition: to lead the world in AI research and to ensure that the technology is developed in a way that aligns with human values.

Thought Leadership and the Broader Impact

Beyond his direct roles in companies like Y Combinator and OpenAI, Altman has become a thought leader whose influence extends far beyond the tech industry.

He is known for his thought-provoking essays and talks on technology, economics, and society. Through his blog, public speaking, and active social media presence, he engages with a broad audience on topics ranging from startup advice to existential risks posed by AI and the future of energy and biotechnology.

Altman is also a strong advocate for universal basic income (UBI), a policy proposal that guarantees a minimum income for all citizens. He sees UBI as a way to address economic inequality and provide a safety net as technological advancements, such as automation, transform the job market. His willingness to champion such forward-thinking ideas illustrates his commitment to not only shaping the future of technology but also considering its broader societal impact.

A Holistic Vision for the Future

What sets Altman apart from many other tech leaders is his holistic approach to innovation. He is not content with merely being at the cutting edge of technology; he also seeks to influence the ethical, regulatory, and economic frameworks that govern technological progress. His career thus far has been characterized by a consistent effort to drive positive change across multiple domains—startups, artificial intelligence, economic policy, and social impact.

Through his work, Altman has demonstrated a profound understanding of the interconnectedness between technology and society. He recognizes that the greatest challenges of the 21st century—climate change, inequality, and global health—cannot be solved by technology alone, but require a combination of innovative solutions, ethical considerations, and forward-looking policies.

Shaping the Next Generation

Altman's influence extends to mentoring and inspiring the next generation of tech entrepreneurs. At Y Combinator, he not only helped startups secure funding but also provided invaluable guidance on navigating the many challenges of building a business. His insights on leadership, decision-making, and growth have shaped the thinking of countless young founders who look to him not just as an investor, but as a mentor who genuinely cares about their success and well-being.

In a world where technology evolves at breakneck speed, Sam Altman has emerged as a visionary leader whose work is shaping the future of industries, economies, and societies. He embodies a rare blend of entrepreneurial spirit, intellectual rigor, and ethical concern, making him a pivotal figure in the tech revolution of our time. As we look to the future, Altman's continued influence will undoubtedly be felt across the globe, driving innovation while addressing the profound questions and challenges that lie ahead.

A Glimpse Into the Journey of Innovation and Influence

Sam Altman's career is a remarkable journey that embodies the intersection of innovation and influence in the fast-moving world of technology. From his beginnings as a curious young tech enthusiast to his emergence as a global leader in artificial intelligence, Altman's story is one of ambition, forward-thinking vision, and an unwavering commitment to using technology to shape the future. His path demonstrates the power of innovation not just as a tool for business success, but as a force for societal transformation.

Early Years: A Passion for Technology

The seeds of Sam Altman's innovation journey were planted early in his life. Born in 1985 in St. Louis, Missouri, Altman exhibited a keen interest in technology from a young age. By the time he was eight years old, he had already learned how to program on his family's computer. This early mastery of technology set the stage for his later accomplishments, but it also reflected something deeper: an innate curiosity about how the world works and how it could be improved through innovation.

For Altman, computers were more than just machines—they were gateways to endless possibilities. As a teenager, he began to explore the potential of technology to solve complex problems, foreshadowing the work he would later do on a much larger scale. His love for technology and his understanding of its transformative power grew as he delved deeper into programming, eventually leading him to Stanford University, where his career in technology would truly begin.

Stanford University: The Birthplace of Ambition

Altman's time at Stanford University was pivotal in shaping his journey of innovation. Enrolling in Stanford's computer science program placed him at the heart of Silicon Valley, the epicenter of global technological innovation. Stanford has long been a breeding ground for some of the world's most successful tech entrepreneurs, and Altman quickly became immersed in this ecosystem of creativity, risk-taking, and entrepreneurial spirit.

At Stanford, Altman gained not only technical knowledge but also exposure to the startup culture that permeated Silicon Valley. He saw firsthand how technological breakthroughs could rapidly scale into billion-dollar companies and how young entrepreneurs were driving innovation in industries ranging from software to biotechnology. This environment sparked Altman's entrepreneurial ambitions, and it wasn't long before he decided to drop out of Stanford to pursue his first major venture—Loopt.

Loopt: The First Steps into the Startup World

In 2005, while still in his early 20s, Sam Altman co-founded Loopt, a location-based social networking app designed to allow users to share their real-time location with friends. Loopt was a product ahead of its time, launching long before location-sharing services like Foursquare or Google Maps became mainstream. Despite the innovative concept and early traction, Loopt faced challenges in gaining widespread adoption. Ultimately, the company was acquired by Green Dot Corporation in 2012 for $43 million.

While Loop did not become the game-changing product Altman had envisioned, it was an invaluable learning experience. It taught him the harsh realities of the startup world—the importance of timing, product-market fit, and user acquisition. More importantly, it introduced him to the inner workings of Silicon Valley, where failure is often seen as a badge of honor and a necessary step toward future success. Altman's first venture into the startup space reinforced his belief in the power of innovation but also sharpened his strategic thinking, which would prove crucial in his next role.

Altman's next chapter would be at Y Combinator (YC), a renowned startup accelerator that was already reshaping Silicon Valley by supporting early-stage companies with seed funding, mentorship, and access to a vast network of investors. YC had helped launch some of the most successful startups of the 21st century, including Airbnb, Dropbox, and Reddit. Recognizing Altman's potential, Paul Graham, the co-founder of YC, invited him to join as a part-time partner in 2011.

Altman's time at YC marked a major turning point in his career. In 2014, he was appointed president of Y Combinator, a role in which he would expand the organization's influence and radically increase the scale of its operations. Under Altman's leadership, YC grew exponentially, funding more startups each year and diversifying its focus to include companies in sectors like biotechnology, clean energy, and artificial intelligence.

Altman's vision for YC was bold and transformative. He saw the organization not just as a startup accelerator, but as an engine for global innovation. By supporting early-stage companies with both capital and guidance, YC became a launchpad for the next generation of entrepreneurs. Altman expanded YC's reach by increasing the number of startups it supported and creating initiatives like YC Continuity, which provided follow-up funding for later-stage companies, and YC Research, which funded ambitious, long-term research projects.

Under Altman's leadership, YC invested in companies that were solving some of the world's most pressing challenges. He believed that true innovation was about more than just building products—it was about creating solutions that could scale and make a meaningful impact on the world. Altman's ability to identify visionary founders and groundbreaking ideas made YC one of the most influential forces in Silicon Valley, helping thousands of startups find their footing and grow into successful, industry-leading companies.

OpenAI: A New Frontier in Artificial Intelligence

As Altman's influence grew, so did his ambitions. After stepping down as YC's president in 2019, he turned his attention to one of the most consequential technologies of our time: artificial intelligence (AI). In 2015, he co-founded OpenAI alongside Elon Musk and several other prominent tech figures. OpenAI's mission was unique: to ensure that artificial intelligence would benefit all of humanity, rather than just a select few.

Unlike most AI research organizations, which often prioritize commercial applications, OpenAI was created as a nonprofit research lab dedicated to advancing AI technology while addressing its ethical implications. Altman and his co-founders understood that AI had the potential to revolutionize industries—from healthcare to transportation—but also carried significant risks. If developed irresponsibly, AI could exacerbate inequality, infringe on privacy, and even pose existential threats to humanity.

At OpenAI, Altman's leadership has been defined by his commitment to responsible innovation. He has overseen the development of cutting-edge AI technologies like GPT-3 and DALL·E, which have demonstrated AI's astonishing capabilities in areas such as language processing, creative content generation, and problem-solving. However, Altman has also been vocal about the need for ethical guidelines and regulatory frameworks to govern AI development. He believes that AI should not only advance technology but also align with human values and benefit society as a whole.

Altman's work at OpenAI reflects his broader philosophy that technology must be developed with careful consideration of its societal impact. He has pushed for transparency in AI research, advocated for government regulation of AI, and led initiatives aimed at democratizing access to advanced AI technologies. Under his guidance, OpenAI has become a leader in the AI space, setting the standard for responsible and ethical AI development.

Thought Leadership and Societal Impact

Sam Altman's journey of influence extends far beyond the startups he has funded or the AI technologies he has developed. He is also a prolific writer and speaker, known for his thought-provoking essays and public talks on technology, economics, and the future of society. Altman's thought leadership often explores the intersection of technology and humanity, with a focus on how innovation can be harnessed to address global challenges like inequality, climate change, and healthcare.

One of Altman's most notable ideas is his advocacy for universal basic income (UBI). He believes that as automation and AI continue to transform the workforce, traditional job markets will be disrupted, leading to widespread unemployment. To address this, Altman has called for the implementation of UBI, which would provide all citizens with a guaranteed income, regardless of employment status. In 2016, Altman even funded an experiment in Oakland, California, to test the feasibility of UBI and gather data on its long-term effects.

Altman's willingness to engage with these complex societal issues reflects his broader vision for the role of technology in shaping the future. He believes that innovation should not be driven solely by profit motives, but by a desire to improve the human condition. By championing ideas like UBI, ethical AI, and global collaboration, Altman has positioned himself as a thought leader who is as concerned with the future of humanity as he is with the future of technology.

The Legacy of a Visionary Leader

Sam Altman's journey of innovation and influence is far from over. He continues to push the boundaries of what's possible, whether through his work at OpenAI, his investments in transformative startups, or his advocacy for policies that promote economic equality and responsible innovation. Altman's influence has reached across multiple sectors, from AI and biotechnology to clean energy and social impact, making him one of the most important figures in the modern tech landscape.

What sets Altman apart is his ability to think not only about technological advancements but also about their broader societal implications. His journey is a testament to the power of visionary leadership and the importance of using innovation as a force for good. As technology continues to reshape the world, Sam Altman's work will serve as a guiding light for those who seek to build a better, more equitable future.

CHAPTER 1: THE EARLY DAYS – FOUNDATIONS OF AN ENTREPRENEUR

Childhood and First Forays Into Technology

Sam Altman's early years were characterized by a fascination with technology and a natural curiosity that set him apart from his peers. Born in 1985 in St. Louis, Missouri, Altman grew up in an environment that fostered intellectual curiosity, though it was far from the tech hubs of Silicon Valley. Despite the geographical distance from the epicenter of innovation, his passion for technology took root at a young age, laying the groundwork for his future in the world of tech entrepreneurship and artificial intelligence.

A Technologically Curious Childhood

Altman's interest in technology began early, spurred by a combination of natural curiosity and access to a family computer. He was about eight years old when he first started exploring how computers worked, a fascination that would shape much of his childhood. Computers at the time were not as user-friendly as they are today, often requiring a certain level of technical understanding even to perform basic tasks. But for Altman, this complexity was not a barrier—it was an invitation to dive deeper.

Unlike many children who might use a computer solely for playing games, Altman's approach was different. He was not content with simply using software; he wanted to understand how it functioned, how it could be modified, and how it could solve problems. He took apart and reassembled hardware, taught himself to code, and experimented with various programming languages. This hands-on learning approach not only sharpened his technical skills but also instilled a sense of confidence in his ability to manipulate technology to create new solutions.

His parents were supportive of his technological interests, providing him with resources and encouragement. This support was crucial, as it allowed him to cultivate his skills without the constraints of a formal learning environment. His self-taught expertise in programming and computer systems would soon translate into an ambition to use technology to solve real-world problems—a hallmark of his later career.

Learning to Program: The Beginning of a Lifelong Passion

Altman's first steps into programming were motivated by a desire to understand how software could control hardware and perform tasks that otherwise seemed impossible. He started with the basics, learning to program in languages like Basic and C, which were commonly used at the time. As he continued to expand his knowledge, he moved on to more complex languages, building programs and experimenting with different types of software.

For Altman, programming was not just a skill but a form of self-expression. It allowed him to bring his ideas to life in a tangible way, turning lines of code into functional programs. This early exposure to programming laid the foundation for his later ventures in the tech world, giving him a solid understanding of how software development works from the ground up.

The internet was also a significant influence during his formative years. In the late 1990s and early 2000s, the internet was rapidly evolving from a niche tool for academics and enthusiasts to a mainstream platform for information, communication, and commerce. Altman, recognizing the potential of this new technology, eagerly explored its capabilities. He taught himself web development and built websites, further solidifying his technological expertise. The internet became a playground for his ideas, allowing him to test and implement various projects, some of which hinted at his future interests in location-based services and social networks.

The Influence of Hobbies and Personal Projects

Sam Altman's childhood was not solely defined by technology, although it certainly played a central role. Like many other children, he pursued a variety of hobbies, but even these often had a technological component. For example, he enjoyed tinkering with electronics, learning how different components interacted, and building rudimentary gadgets. This hands-on experience with hardware complemented his programming skills and gave him a broader understanding of how software and hardware could be integrated to create innovative solutions.

His projects during this time were small but significant. These early experiments often involved writing code to solve simple problems or to automate tasks that interested him. For instance, he might write a program to simulate a game or automate a repetitive process on the computer. These projects were not just exercises in programming; they were practical lessons in problem-solving and innovation. Each new project presented unique challenges, teaching him to think critically and develop solutions—a mindset that would later become essential in his entrepreneurial endeavors.

The blend of curiosity, experimentation, and technical skill that characterized Altman's childhood projects laid the groundwork for his later ventures. It cultivated an approach to learning that prioritized exploration and iterative improvement, rather than strict adherence to formal education. This self-driven learning style would become a defining feature of his career, as he often ventured into uncharted territory with confidence and a willingness to learn from failure.

The Drive to Create: Building on Early Interests

From a young age, Altman demonstrated a strong desire to create and innovate. While many children are content to play with toys, he preferred to build his own. His inclination toward creation rather than consumption was evident in his approach to technology, where he was always more interested in developing new tools than in merely using existing ones. This drive to create extended beyond just programming; it was a broader desire to solve problems, improve systems, and make things more efficient.

Altman's early projects often revolved around finding ways to make tasks easier or more enjoyable, reflecting a mindset that saw technology as a means of improving life rather than merely serving as a pastime. This perspective would later manifest in his ventures, such as Loopt, a location-based social networking app, which he would co-found as a young adult. The roots of such projects were evident in his childhood experiments, where he sought to leverage technology to create new experiences and solve practical problems.

The Role of Education: Balancing Formal Learning and Self-Exploration

While Sam Altman attended traditional schools, much of his technological education occurred outside the classroom. He found that the structure of formal education sometimes limited his ability to explore his interests in depth. This was particularly true in subjects like computer science, where the curriculum was often outdated or too rigid for someone who was already programming independently.

Altman's educational experiences shaped his views on learning. He believed in the importance of self-driven education, where students pursue topics they are passionate about and learn through experimentation. This approach not only fueled his own learning but also informed his later work in fostering innovation and entrepreneurship through Y Combinator, where he emphasized hands-on problem-solving over formal training.

His time at high school, and later at Stanford University, reinforced the idea that while formal education could provide a foundation, real learning often took place outside traditional classrooms. At Stanford, he briefly studied computer science before deciding to drop out and pursue his entrepreneurial interests full-time. The decision to leave Stanford was not an indictment of the value of education but rather a recognition that his own learning and growth would be better served by working on real-world projects. It was a decision that would ultimately set the stage for his future success.

The Early Lessons That Shaped His Mindset

The lessons Altman learned in his childhood and adolescence laid a strong foundation for his later success. Several key themes emerged from these early experiences:

Curiosity as a Driver of Learning: Altman's desire to understand how things worked motivated him to learn programming and explore different aspects of technology. This curiosity-driven approach to learning enabled him to acquire skills that were not part of any formal curriculum.

Problem-Solving Mindset: From an early age, he was interested in finding solutions to problems, whether they were small tasks or larger challenges. This mindset would be crucial in his later entrepreneurial ventures, where solving problems for users would be at the heart of his business strategies.

Embracing Failure as a Learning Tool: The projects Altman undertook as a child did not always succeed, but each failure was a learning opportunity. This resilience and willingness to learn from mistakes would later help him navigate the uncertainties of the startup world.

Hands-On Experience Over Theoretical Knowledge: While Altman valued education, he often found that hands-on experimentation taught him more than traditional classroom settings. This practical approach to learning influenced his decision to drop out of Stanford and pursue real-world projects, and it would also shape his philosophy when mentoring startups at Y Combinator.

Setting the Stage for a Technological Journey

By the time Altman reached adulthood, he had already developed a deep understanding of technology and a passion for using it to create solutions. His early experiences with computers, programming, and personal projects instilled in him the skills and mindset necessary to thrive in the tech world. These foundational experiences not only prepared him for his first entrepreneurial venture, Loopt, but also for his future role as a leader in the world of startups and artificial intelligence.

Sam Altman's childhood was more than just a period of learning; it was the beginning of a lifelong journey of innovation. The lessons he learned and the skills he developed would go on to influence not only his career trajectory but also his approach to leadership, entrepreneurship, and technological advancement. His early forays into technology laid the groundwork for a life dedicated to shaping the future, one innovation at a time.

Discovering the Spirit of Innovation

Sam Altman's path to becoming a transformative figure in the tech world was driven by his discovery and cultivation of the spirit of innovation. This spirit, which became evident early in his life, guided him through his formative years and continued to shape his professional journey. Altman's ability to identify opportunities, challenge conventional wisdom, and pursue groundbreaking ideas set him apart as an innovator with a mission to shape the future. The spirit of innovation was not merely about creating new products or services for him; it was about fundamentally changing how technology could be used to solve real-world problems and improve lives.

The Early Seeds of Innovation

Altman's childhood experiences laid the foundation for his innovative mindset. Growing up in St. Louis,

Missouri, he was not surrounded by the tech culture that permeated Silicon Valley, but his curiosity about technology was constant. The family computer became his first laboratory, where he experimented with programming languages, took apart and reassembled hardware, and built simple applications. These experiences were more than just hobbies; they represented an early stage of discovery that was deeply intertwined with his emerging spirit of innovation.

He developed a passion for understanding how things worked and, more importantly, how they could be improved. This mindset was integral to discovering the spirit of innovation because it emphasized not just the joy of learning, but also the desire to create something new. The recognition that he could use technology to solve problems, even in small ways, gave him a sense of empowerment and laid the groundwork for a career focused on technological advancements.

Formative Experiences: Learning to Innovate Through Failure

The spirit of innovation is often nurtured through trial and error, and Altman was no stranger to failure. In his early experiments with software development, not every project succeeded, but each attempt brought valuable lessons. This period of trial and error helped him develop a key aspect of his innovative approach: resilience. He learned to view failure not as a setback but as a stepping stone toward success.

Failure taught him to iterate and refine his ideas continuously. He understood that true innovation often requires multiple iterations, each bringing him closer to a viable solution. This resilience became a hallmark of his later work, where he encouraged a culture of experimentation and learning, whether at Y Combinator or in his ventures like OpenAI. For Altman, the spirit of innovation was inseparable from the willingness to embrace uncertainty and learn from mistakes.

The Impact of Stanford University: Fostering a Culture of Innovation

When Altman enrolled at Stanford University to study computer science, he found himself at the heart of Silicon Valley—a region synonymous with technological innovation and entrepreneurship. The culture at Stanford exposed him to a world where groundbreaking ideas were not only encouraged but also expected. Here, Altman encountered peers and mentors who shared his passion for technology and who were actively engaged in pushing the boundaries of what was possible.

Stanford's unique environment, with its close ties to the tech industry, was a catalyst for Altman's innovative spirit. The university served as a launchpad where students were not only taught about technology but also challenged to apply their knowledge in new and creative ways. Altman took advantage of this culture, often engaging in side projects and experiments outside of his formal coursework. His experience at Stanford fostered his desire to start his own company, leading him to co-found Loopt while still a student.

Dropping out of Stanford to pursue Loopt was a bold decision, but it was driven by his confidence in the power of innovation to transform industries. He was not content to merely study computer science; he wanted to apply his knowledge to solve real-world problems. This decision marked a significant moment in Altman's journey—one where the spirit of innovation transformed from a personal mindset into a professional mission.

Loopt: The First Major Step Toward Innovation

Co-founding Loopt in 2005 represented Altman's first significant foray into the tech startup world. Loopt was a location-based social networking app that allowed users to share their real-time location with friends, offering a new way to connect socially and explore nearby points of interest. At a time when smartphones were still relatively new, and GPS technology was just beginning to gain traction, Loopt was ahead of the curve.

The app's concept reflected Altman's belief in using technology to bring people closer together and make life more convenient. Although Loopt did not achieve the massive success he had hoped for, ultimately being acquired by Green Dot Corporation in 2012, it was a crucial learning experience. The company's challenges taught Altman valuable lessons about product-market fit, timing, and the difficulties of scaling a new technology. More importantly, Loopt helped him discover that innovation often involves navigating uncharted territory, where risks are high but so are the rewards.

Loopt demonstrated the power of bold ideas and the need for adaptability in the face of changing market dynamics. The experience reaffirmed Altman's commitment to entrepreneurship and laid the groundwork for his later involvement with Y Combinator, where he would go on to help other startups navigate similar challenges.

Y Combinator: Scaling the Spirit of Innovation

Altman's tenure at Y Combinator (YC) marked a new phase in his journey, where he transitioned from being an entrepreneur to a mentor and investor. Y Combinator was already known as one of the world's leading startup accelerators, having supported successful companies like Dropbox, Airbnb, and Reddit. Altman's appointment as president in 2014 was a testament to his reputation for fostering innovation, and his leadership would significantly expand YC's influence.

At Y Combinator, Altman championed a culture that encouraged bold ideas and rapid experimentation. He believed in providing startups with not just capital, but also the mentorship and support needed to transform innovative ideas into successful businesses. Under his leadership, YC grew substantially, funding more startups each year and expanding its focus beyond software to include sectors like biotechnology, clean energy, and artificial intelligence.

Altman's vision for YC was about more than just scaling startups; it was about scaling the spirit of innovation itself. He emphasized that innovation was not limited to technology companies, but could be applied to any field where new ideas had the potential to drive progress. By broadening YC's scope and creating programs like YC Continuity (which provided follow-on funding to later-stage companies) and YC Research (which focused on long-term projects with broad societal impact), Altman fostered an environment where innovators could pursue ambitious goals without being constrained by conventional thinking.

Embracing the Long-Term Vision: Ethical and Societal Impacts of Innovation

Altman's journey in discovering the spirit of innovation was also marked by a growing awareness of the broader societal implications of technological advancements. He understood that true innovation could not be solely defined by financial success or technological breakthroughs. It also had to consider the ethical implications and potential impacts on society. This awareness was particularly evident in his work at OpenAI, an organization he co-founded in 2015 to advance artificial intelligence in a way that would be beneficial for all of humanity.

At OpenAI, Altman pursued a vision of responsible innovation. He recognized that while I had the potential to revolutionize industries and improve lives, it also posed significant risks if not developed with caution and ethical considerations in mind. OpenAI's mission to ensure that artificial general intelligence (AGI) benefits humanity reflects Altman's belief that innovation should be guided by principles that prioritize the greater good.

His advocacy for ethical AI development, transparency in AI research, and collaboration between the private sector and governments underscored his commitment to using innovation as a force for positive change. He pushed for regulatory frameworks to govern AI, emphasizing that companies and governments needed to work together to address the challenges and risks posed by rapidly advancing technology.

Encouraging a Culture of Innovation: Altman's Broader Influence

Altman's influence extends beyond the startups he has supported or the technologies he has helped develop. He has become a prominent advocate for fostering a culture of innovation that is accessible to a wide range of people, regardless of their background or location. His thought leadership, expressed through essays, public talks, and social media, often emphasizes the need for an entrepreneurial mindset that is not constrained by traditional boundaries.

He advocates for policies that enable more people to participate in the innovation economy, such as universal basic income (UBI), which he sees as a potential solution to the economic disruptions caused by automation and AI. His support for UBI reflects his understanding that innovation can lead to significant changes in the workforce, and society must be prepared to adapt.

Altman's broader vision includes democratizing access to technology and entrepreneurship. He has pushed for initiatives that make startup resources more accessible to people around the world, ensuring that the spirit of innovation is not confined to Silicon Valley but spread across different regions and communities. This approach aligns with his belief that diverse perspectives can drive more meaningful and inclusive technological advancements.

The Legacy of an Innovator

Discovering the spirit of innovation was not a one-time event for Sam Altman; it was a continuous process of learning, adapting, and expanding his vision. From his early experiments with computers to leading major organizations like Y Combinator and OpenAI, Altman's journey reflects a lifelong commitment to using technology as a means of solving problems and driving progress. His story illustrates that innovation is not just about inventing new products or founding startups—it is about challenging existing paradigms, thinking long-term, and striving to make a positive impact on society.

Sam Altman's legacy as an innovator is still unfolding, but his influence is already evident in the numerous companies he has mentored, the technologies he has helped develop, and the conversations he has sparked about the future of technology and society. The spirit of innovation that he discovered early in life continues to guide his efforts, inspiring a new generation of entrepreneurs to think boldly and act with purpose.

The Leap Into Startups: Loopt and the Lessons Learned

Sam Altman's first significant entrepreneurial endeavor came with the founding of Loopt, a location-based social networking app that would pave the way for his future in tech startups. Loopt, launched in 2005, was a pioneering attempt to leverage mobile technology and location data to enhance social interaction. The experience of building, scaling, and eventually selling Loopt provided Altman with invaluable lessons in entrepreneurship, technology, and the art of navigating the startup world. It was a journey marked by early promise, challenges, and ultimately, insights that would shape his career and influence his approach to helping other entrepreneurs through Y Combinator.

The Birth of Loopt: Identifying a Need in the Market

The concept for Loopt emerged while Altman was still a student at Stanford University, where he was studying computer science. Like many of his peers, he was fascinated by the potential of emerging technologies to transform everyday life. During this time, the mobile phone was beginning to evolve from a simple communication device into a multi-functional tool with increasing capabilities. The introduction of the iPhone in 2007 would later accelerate this shift, but even before that, GPS technology was becoming more accessible to consumers, providing a new frontier for innovation.

Altman and his co-founders saw an opportunity to combine GPS technology with social networking to create a location-based service that allowed users to share their real-time location with friends. The goal was to make it easier for people to find each other, coordinate social activities, and discover nearby points of interest. At its core, Loopt aimed to bring the online social experience into the physical world, bridging the gap between digital connections and real-life interactions.

The idea was ahead of its time in many ways, anticipating the widespread use of location-based services that would later become commonplace with apps like Foursquare, Snapchat, and even Google Maps' location-sharing features. In 2005, however, the concept was novel, and the market was still in its infancy. Loopt sought to capitalize on this emerging trend by being one of the first apps to use location data as the primary driver for social interaction.

Early Success: Securing Funding and Building the Team

As a young startup, Loopt quickly gained attention in the tech community, especially in Silicon Valley, where there was growing interest in mobile applications and social networks. Altman's decision to drop out of Stanford to pursue Loopt full-time was a bold move, but it paid off early when the company was accepted into the inaugural batch of Y Combinator (YC), the startup accelerator co-founded by Paul Graham.

Being part of Y Combinator was a significant boost for Loopt. The program provided not only seed funding but also mentorship and connections that were crucial for a young company trying to establish itself. Y Combinator's network of investors and advisors helped Altman and his team refine their product, develop a go-to-market strategy, and secure additional funding. Loopt attracted investment from major venture capital firms, including Sequoia Capital, signaling strong market interest and giving the startup the financial resources to grow.

The funding allowed Loopt to expand its team and invest in product development. Altman assembled a group of talented engineers and designers who were excited about the potential of location-based technology. Together, they worked on building a robust platform that could support the app's features and scale as the user base grew. The company was one of the first to have its app pre-installed on mobile phones through partnerships with carriers, giving it early visibility and adoption in the nascent mobile app market.

Navigating the Challenges: Product-Market Fit and User Adoption

Despite early enthusiasm and funding, Loopt faced significant challenges that tested Altman's skills as an entrepreneur. One of the most pressing issues was achieving product-market fit. While the idea of sharing one's location with friends was innovative, it required users to change their behavior and adopt a new way of thinking about social interaction. The concept of continuously sharing one's real-time location raised privacy concerns and made some users uncomfortable, limiting the app's widespread adoption.

Furthermore, the mobile ecosystem in the mid-2000s was not as mature as it is today. Smartphones were still evolving, and data plans were relatively expensive, which affected the ability of users to fully utilize Loopy's features. The app's reliance on GPS technology also meant that it drained phone batteries quickly, presenting another barrier to regular use. These technical limitations made it challenging for Loopt to deliver a seamless and compelling user experience, especially when compared to the social networks and services that were purely web-based at the time.

Loopt tried to address these challenges through various iterations of its product, adding new features such as event discovery, location-based alerts, and rewards for checking into specific locations. However, user adoption continued to be slower than anticipated. While Loop did manage to attract a dedicated group of users, it struggled to achieve the kind of viral growth that startups like Facebook and Twitter were experiencing during the same period.

The Reality Check: Competing in a Crowded Market

As the mobile app ecosystem grew, so did the number of competitors in the location-based services space. Companies like Foursquare and Gowalla entered the market with similar ideas but with different approaches to engaging users. Foursquare, for example, introduced the concept of "checking in" to locations and earning badges, which gamified the experience and helped the app gain traction among a broader audience. The increasing competition highlighted the difficulty of differentiating Loopt in a market that was rapidly evolving.

Additionally, larger companies such as Google and Facebook began incorporating location-based features into their platforms, leveraging their existing user bases to provide similar services. These giants had the resources to iterate quickly and the advantage of established networks, making it harder for a standalone app like Loopt to compete. This market shift forced Altman and his team to reassess their strategy and consider whether Loopt could continue to grow as an independent company.

The reality was that despite Loopy's early promise and the significant resources invested, it was not able to achieve the level of success that Altman had envisioned. The startup's struggles to scale effectively and compete in a crowded space became apparent, leading to a critical juncture in the company’s journey.

The Acquisition by Green Dot Corporation: An Exit Strategy

In 2012, after several years of trying to scale Loopt and pivot the product to find the right market fit, the company was acquired by Green Dot Corporation for $43.4 million. Green Dot, a financial technology company best known for its prepaid debit cards, was interested in Loopy's technology to enhance its mobile banking and financial services offerings. For Altman, the acquisition represented a strategic exit that allowed the team to transition to new opportunities while recouping some of the investment made in the company. Although Loopt did not achieve the massive consumer success that some other startups did, the acquisition was a valuable learning experience for Altman. It taught him important lessons about the startup lifecycle, market timing, and the competitive nature of the tech industry. These lessons would later influence his approach at Y Combinator, where he would mentor other entrepreneurs on the importance of understanding market dynamics and being willing to pivot or pursue exits when necessary.

Key Lessons Learned from Loopt

The Importance of Timing and Market Readiness: One of the major takeaways from Loopt was the significance of timing in the success of a tech startup. While the idea of location-based social networking was ahead of its time, the market and technology were not fully ready to support widespread adoption. GPS technology was still relatively new, smartphones had not yet reached full market penetration, and users were not entirely comfortable with sharing their location data. This experience taught Altman that even a great idea needs the right market conditions to thrive.

Achieving Product-Market Fit: The challenge of finding product-market fit was a central issue for Loopt. Despite multiple iterations and feature additions, the app struggled to resonate with a broad user base. This underscored the importance of not just building a technically sound product, but also ensuring that it solves a real problem for a large audience. For future endeavors, Altman emphasized the need to focus on user needs and adapt products based on feedback and usage patterns.

Navigating Competition and Differentiation: The emergence of strong competitors like Foursquare and the entry of tech giants into the location-based services space demonstrated the importance of differentiation in a competitive market. Loopy's experience showed Altman that startups must be agile and innovative to stay ahead of rivals, and that simply being first to market does not guarantee success. Effective branding, unique value propositions, and understanding competitors' strengths and weaknesses became critical lessons.

Adaptability and Knowing When to Exit: Loopy's journey taught Altman about the need for adaptability in business strategy. The company tried different approaches to improve user engagement, from location-based alerts to partnerships with telecom companies, but ultimately, it was clear that a different path was needed. The acquisition by Green Dot was a pragmatic decision that allowed Loopt to exit gracefully while providing value to its investors and team members. This lesson reinforced the idea that sometimes, knowing when to exit or pivot is just as important as knowing how to grow.

Leveraging Networks and Mentorship: Y Combinator's support played a crucial role in Loopy's early development, providing seed funding, mentorship, and connections. This experience underscored the value of networks and guidance in the startup world. Altman would later apply this understanding to his leadership at Y Combinator, where he focused on building an ecosystem that offered startups more than just financial investment.

How Loopt Shaped Altman's Future Ventures

The lessons learned from Loopt significantly shaped Altman's approach to future ventures. When he took on leadership roles at Y Combinator and later co-founded OpenAI, he brought with him a deep understanding of the challenges that startups face. His experiences helped him develop a more empathetic and pragmatic approach to mentoring other entrepreneurs, advising them not only on achieving growth but also on navigating the complex realities of building a business.

At Y Combinator, Altman encouraged a culture of rapid iteration and continuous learning, values that he had embraced during his time with Loopt. He was open about his experiences, sharing insights on the importance of timing, product-market fit, and knowing when to make strategic exits. This transparency helped build trust with the startups in the accelerator program, as they saw him not just as a mentor, but as someone who had faced similar struggles and emerged wiser from the experience.

Moreover, Let's focus on mobile technology and social networking influenced Altman's later work in artificial intelligence and other fields. He became particularly interested in technologies with the potential for significant societal impact, such as AI, where ethical considerations and market readiness play crucial roles. The journey with Loopt had shown him that technology must be developed with a long-term vision in mind, considering not just the immediate market but also future implications.

Sam Altman's leap into the world of startups with Loopt was a foundational experience that shaped his career as an entrepreneur, mentor, and investor. While the company did not achieve the blockbuster success that some other startups did, the journey provided invaluable lessons about market timing, product development, competition, and strategic decision-making. These insights became instrumental in Altman's later work, particularly at Y Combinator, where he applied the lessons learned to help other entrepreneurs navigate the complexities of building successful startups.

Loopy's story is a testament to the fact that not all entrepreneurial ventures result in massive success, but even the less-than-perfect outcomes can be rich with learning and growth opportunities. For Altman, Loopt was more than just a startup; it was a learning ground that prepared him for future endeavors, enabling him to make a more significant impact on the tech industry and beyond.

CHAPTER 2: MASTERING THE ART OF STARTUPS – Y COMBINATOR ERA

Joining Y Combinator: A Turning Point

Sam Altman's journey through the tech startup landscape reached a pivotal moment when he joined Y Combinator (YC), the esteemed startup accelerator co-founded by Paul Graham. This transition from entrepreneur to mentor and leader marked a significant turning point in Altman's career, shaping not only his future but also the trajectory of countless startups that would go through the program. By immersing himself in the vibrant ecosystem of Y Combinator, Altman gained invaluable insights, expanded his network, and adopted a mentorship approach that would influence a generation of entrepreneurs.

The Inception of Y Combinator

Founded in 2005, Y Combinator was created to provide early-stage startups with seed funding, mentorship, and a structured program to refine their ideas. The innovative model focused on small batches of startups that could benefit from hands-on support, networking opportunities, and direct access to investors. Paul Graham, a renowned computer scientist and entrepreneur, envisioned a space where talented individuals could pursue their entrepreneurial dreams with the resources and guidance needed to succeed.

From its inception, Y Combinator became synonymous with startup success stories, nurturing companies like Airbnb, Dropbox, Reddit, and Stripe. The accelerator's unique approach and focus on fostering innovation quickly garnered attention within the tech community, establishing YC as a launching pad for ambitious entrepreneurs. As the organization grew, it began to attract an increasing number of applicants seeking to join its ranks and take advantage of its resources.

Sam Altman's Entry into Y Combinator

Altman's association with Y Combinator began as a participant when he co-founded Loopt and was accepted into the inaugural batch of the program in 2005. The accelerator's support was instrumental in getting Loopt off the ground, providing seed funding, mentorship, and critical connections that helped the young startup navigate the competitive landscape of tech entrepreneurship.

However, it was in 2014 that Altman's relationship with Y Combinator deepened when he was appointed as president. This transition marked a turning point not only for Altman but also for the organization itself. His experience as a startup founder provided him with a unique perspective on the challenges entrepreneurs face, enabling him to empathize with and effectively guide the next generation of innovators.

A New Vision for Y Combinator

As president, Altman sought to expand Y Combinator's influence and reach, while also enhancing its core mission of supporting startups. One of his first initiatives was to increase the number of companies accepted into each batch, reflecting his belief that a greater diversity of ideas and entrepreneurs would ultimately lead to more innovation. Under his leadership, the accelerator's annual funding amount also increased, allowing startups to secure the financial backing necessary to pursue their visions with greater confidence.

Altman implemented a more structured curriculum that emphasized not only product development and market fit but also the importance of building a strong company culture. He understood that successful startups require more than just great ideas; they need resilient teams that can adapt to challenges and grow together. By prioritizing mentorship, Altman fostered an environment where founders could learn from one another, share experiences, and collectively navigate the ups and downs of entrepreneurship.

Fostering a Culture of Experimentation and Iteration

One of Altman's key contributions to Y Combinator was the encouragement of a culture that embraced experimentation and iteration. Drawing from his own experiences with Loopt, where failure was an essential part of the learning process, he emphasized the importance of agility in the startup world. Founders were encouraged to test their ideas quickly, gather user feedback, and iterate on their products based on real-world data.

This approach resonated deeply with the core principles of Silicon Valley, where rapid prototyping and customer-driven development have become the norm.

Altman's advocacy for an experimental mindset helped demystify the process of building a startup, making it clear that even the most successful entrepreneurs face setbacks along the way. He reinforced the notion that innovation often emerges from trial and error, urging founders to embrace their failures as valuable learning opportunities rather than insurmountable obstacles.

Expanding the Reach of Y Combinator

Under Altman's leadership, Y Combinator expanded its reach beyond traditional tech startups. He recognized that innovation could occur in various sectors, including healthcare, biotechnology, education, and even energy. This broader focus allowed YC to attract a diverse array of startups with unique approaches to solving pressing global challenges.

The launch of programs such as YC Continuity, which provided follow-on funding to later-stage companies, and YC Research, aimed at supporting long-term research projects, showcased Altman's commitment to nurturing a wider range of ideas. By investing in companies across different stages and industries, Y Combinator solidified its reputation as a breeding ground for innovation and experimentation.

The Impact of Mentorship and Community

One of the hallmarks of Y Combinator is its emphasis on community, and Altman recognized the power of mentorship in fostering collaboration among entrepreneurs. He encouraged successful alumni to engage with current founders, sharing insights and experiences that could help navigate the complexities of startup life. This mentoring network became a vital resource, allowing newer entrepreneurs to tap into a wealth of knowledge from those who had walked similar paths.

The connections made through Y Combinator often led to lasting partnerships and collaborations, reinforcing the idea that entrepreneurship is not a solitary endeavor but rather a collective journey. Altman understood that building a supportive ecosystem was essential for fostering innovation, and he actively promoted opportunities for alumni to connect and collaborate through events, workshops, and networking opportunities.

OpenAI: A Vision for Responsible Innovation

In addition to his work at Y Combinator, Altman co-founded OpenAI in 2015, which reflects his commitment to advancing artificial intelligence in a manner that benefits humanity. His experience at Y Combinator reinforced the importance of ethical considerations in technological innovation. He recognized that as AI technologies rapidly advanced, it was crucial to develop frameworks that ensure their responsible deployment.

OpenAI's objective to ensure that artificial general intelligence (AGI) benefits all of humankind is consistent with Altman's vision of using technology for the greater good. The organization emphasizes transparency, safety, and collaboration with the broader AI research community to mitigate the risks associated with powerful technologies. This focus on responsible innovation is rooted in the lessons Altman learned throughout his entrepreneurial journey, particularly during his time at Y Combinator.

Lessons Learned from Joining Y Combinator

The Value of Mentorship and Community: Altman's experiences at Y Combinator highlighted the importance of mentorship and community in entrepreneurship. The support and guidance provided by experienced founders and investors can be invaluable, helping new entrepreneurs navigate challenges and avoid common pitfalls. Building strong relationships within the startup community can lead to collaborative opportunities and shared learning experiences.

Embracing Experimentation and Iteration: Altman's emphasis on experimentation and iteration underscored the need for startups to adopt an agile mindset. Rapid testing, user feedback, and adaptation are crucial for achieving product-market fit and ensuring that startups can pivot when necessary. This approach encourages a culture of continuous improvement, where failure is seen as a stepping stone to success.

Broadening the Scope of Innovation: Altman recognized that innovation is not confined to traditional tech sectors. By encouraging startups from various industries, he demonstrated that transformative ideas can emerge in diverse fields. This broadening of focus allows for creative solutions to complex challenges and fosters a more inclusive entrepreneurial ecosystem.

Building Resilient Teams and Cultures: Altman's time at YC made the importance of company culture evident. Successful startups require teams that are aligned in vision and values and capable of navigating challenges together. Cultivating a positive culture of collaboration, trust, and shared purpose is vital for long-term success.

Responsible Innovation: Altman's work with OpenAI reinforced the need for ethical considerations in technology development. As startups push boundaries and explore new frontiers, it is essential to consider the societal implications of their innovations. Responsible leadership and ethical frameworks are critical for ensuring that technology serves the greater good.

Joining Y Combinator marked a transformative turning point for Sam Altman, shifting his role from entrepreneur to leader, mentor, and advocate for innovation. His experiences within the accelerator shaped not only his approach to entrepreneurship but also the trajectory of countless startups that benefited from YC's resources and community.

Under Altman's leadership, Y Combinator evolved into a more inclusive and expansive accelerator, fostering a culture of experimentation and collaboration. His commitment to responsible innovation, mentorship, and community-building has left a lasting impact on the startup ecosystem, shaping the next generation of entrepreneurs as they strive to navigate the complexities of building successful businesses. As Altman continues to influence the tech landscape, the lessons learned during his time at Y Combinator will resonate for years to come, inspiring future innovators to pursue their visions with confidence and purpose.

Scaling Startups: The Art of Nurturing Innovation

Scaling a startup is one of the most challenging yet rewarding phases of entrepreneurial growth. It involves transforming a fledgling idea into a sustainable and thriving business capable of significant impact. For Sam Altman, his leadership at Y Combinator (YC) and experiences with various startups have offered profound insights into the nuances of nurturing innovation during this critical stage. This extensive exploration delves into the art of scaling startups, focusing on the principles, challenges, strategies, and mindset required to navigate the complex journey of growth.

Understanding the Need for Scaling

Scaling refers to the process of increasing a startup's capacity to generate revenue while managing costs effectively. This is distinct from mere growth, which can often be achieved through increased spending or unsustainable practices. True scaling requires a startup to optimize its operations, refine its business model, and ensure that it can meet rising demand without compromising quality or customer satisfaction.

For many entrepreneurs, the need to scale arises from various factors:

Market Demand: As a product gains traction, the demand for it may exceed the startup's current capacity, necessitating a scale-up to meet customer needs.

Competition: In a fast-paced tech landscape, competitors are constantly vying for market share. Scaling effectively allows startups to stay ahead and maintain a competitive edge.

Investment Opportunities: Investors typically seek scalable business models, making it essential for startups to demonstrate their potential for rapid growth to secure funding.

Vision and Impact: Many founders are motivated by a desire to create meaningful change. Scaling their startups allows them to amplify their impact on society, industry, or specific markets.

The Role of Culture in Scaling

One of the most crucial aspects of scaling a startup is fostering a strong organizational culture that supports innovation and collaboration. The culture of a startup is often its backbone; it shapes how employees interact, make decisions, and approach challenges. As startups grow, maintaining a healthy culture becomes increasingly vital to retain talent and sustain motivation.

Encouraging a Growth Mindset

A growth mindset, a concept popularized by psychologist Carol Dweck, refers to the belief that abilities and intelligence can be developed through hard work and dedication. Encouraging this mindset within a startup fosters resilience and adaptability. Founders should promote continuous learning, embrace failures as learning opportunities, and celebrate achievements to cultivate an environment where innovation thrives.

Fostering Open Communication

Open communication is essential in a scaling startup, as it encourages transparency and trust among team members. As teams grow, maintaining clear lines of communication can become challenging. Implementing regular check-ins, feedback loops, and collaborative platforms helps ensure that all team members are aligned with the company's goals and feel valued in their contributions.

Building Diverse Teams

Diversity within teams fosters creativity and innovation. Different perspectives can lead to unique solutions and approaches to problems. Scaling startups should prioritize building diverse teams that reflect various backgrounds, experiences, and skill sets. This diversity can enhance problem-solving capabilities and drive more effective decision-making.

Product-Market Fit: The Foundation of Scaling

Achieving product-market fit (PMF) is a prerequisite for any startup looking to scale. PMF occurs when a product satisfies a strong market demand, leading to sustainable customer engagement and growth. Without PMF, scaling efforts may lead to wasted resources and potential failure.

Identifying Customer Needs

Startups should continually seek to understand their customers' evolving needs and preferences. This can involve conducting surveys, engaging with users, and analyzing data to identify trends and pain points. By prioritizing customer feedback, startups can iterate on their products to enhance value and ensure they resonate with the target audience.

Iterating Quickly

In the startup world, speed is essential. The ability to iterate quickly based on customer feedback and market trends allows startups to refine their offerings and maintain relevance. Adopting an agile development process, which emphasizes rapid prototyping and incremental improvements, can accelerate the journey toward achieving PMF.

Validating Assumptions

As startups scale, they often encounter assumptions about their market, product, or customer behavior. Validating these assumptions through experiments and data analysis is critical to ensure that scaling efforts are grounded in reality. This involves running A/B tests, gathering user feedback, and analyzing performance metrics to make informed decisions.

Funding and Resources: Fueling the Scale-Up

Scaling requires significant financial resources to invest in technology, talent, marketing, and infrastructure. As startups seek to scale, they often explore various funding options to secure the capital needed for growth.

Venture Capital

Venture capital (VC) funding is a popular avenue for startups looking to scale quickly. VC firms provide capital in exchange for equity and typically offer mentorship and strategic guidance. Startups must be prepared to present a compelling business case, demonstrate traction, and outline their growth plans to attract VC investment.

Bootstrapping

Some entrepreneurs choose to bootstrap their startups, relying on personal savings and revenue generated by the business. This approach allows founders to retain full ownership and control but may limit the speed of scaling. Bootstrapping requires careful financial management and a focus on sustainable growth to ensure that the startup can fund its expansion without external support.

Alternative Funding Sources

In addition to traditional VC funding, startups can explore alternative financing options, such as crowdfunding, angel investors, or government grants.

These avenues can provide the necessary capital while also validating market interest in the startup's product or service.

Building Scalable Operations

As startups scale, operational efficiency becomes paramount. Founders must implement processes and systems that enable the organization to manage increased demand without sacrificing quality.

Streamlining Processes

Startups should regularly assess and optimize their internal processes to eliminate bottlenecks and enhance productivity. This can involve automating repetitive tasks, adopting project management tools, and creating standardized workflows. Streamlining operations allows teams to focus on high-value activities that drive innovation.

Investing in Technology

Technology plays a critical role in scaling operations. Investing in scalable solutions, such as cloud-based platforms, customer relationship management (CRM) systems, and analytics tools, enables startups to manage their growth effectively. These technologies provide insights into customer behavior, operational performance, and market trends, allowing founders to make data-driven decisions.

Hiring Strategically

As startups scale, hiring becomes increasingly important. Building a talented and adaptable team is essential for driving innovation and managing growth. Founders should prioritize hiring individuals who align with the company's values and possess the skills needed to contribute to the startup's success. Creating a strong onboarding process helps ensure that new hires quickly integrate into the culture and contribute to team dynamics.

Nurturing Innovation During Growth

As startups scale, the challenge lies in maintaining the innovative spirit that drove their initial success. Founders must actively nurture a culture of innovation to ensure that the organization continues to evolve and adapt.

Encouraging Experimentation

Encouraging teams to experiment with new ideas and approaches fosters a culture of innovation. This can involve allocating resources for research and development, hosting hackathons, or providing time for employees to pursue passion projects. By creating an environment where experimentation is valued, startups can uncover new opportunities and drive growth.

Establishing Innovation Processes

While spontaneity is vital for innovation, establishing structured processes for generating and evaluating ideas can enhance creativity within the organization. This may involve setting up cross-functional teams to brainstorm solutions, conducting regular innovation workshops, or implementing idea management systems that allow employees to submit and refine concepts.

Recognizing and Rewarding Innovation

Celebrating innovative contributions is essential for reinforcing a culture of creativity. Founders should recognize individuals or teams who propose and implement innovative solutions, whether through formal awards or informal shout-outs. This recognition encourages others to think creatively and contributes to a positive work environment.

Navigating Challenges in Scaling

Scaling is not without its challenges, and founders must be prepared to navigate obstacles that may arise during the process.

Managing Growing Pains

As startups grow, they may encounter challenges related to communication, team dynamics, and operational efficiency. Founders must be proactive in addressing these growing pains, fostering open discussions, and implementing solutions that ensure the organization can continue to function cohesively.

Maintaining Quality Control

With increased production and customer demand, maintaining quality control becomes paramount. Founders should implement systems to monitor product quality, gather customer feedback, and respond swiftly to any issues. Quality assurance processes help protect the startup's reputation and ensure customer satisfaction.

Balancing Short-Term and Long-Term Goals

Startups frequently confront the challenge of reconciling short-term financial needs with long-term strategic objectives.While it may be tempting to prioritize immediate revenue generation, founders should remain focused on building a sustainable business that can withstand market fluctuations. This requires careful planning and a commitment to the company's vision.

The Future of Scaling Startups

As the tech landscape continues to evolve, the approach to scaling startups will also shift. Emerging technologies, changing consumer behaviors, and global challenges will shape the future of entrepreneurship. Founders must remain adaptable and open to new ideas, recognizing that scaling is an ongoing process rather than a destination.

Embracing Sustainability: The growing emphasis on sustainability and social responsibility will impact how startups scale. Founders must consider the environmental and societal implications of their growth strategies, integrating sustainability into their business models.

Leveraging Data and Analytics: The increasing availability of data will empower startups to make informed decisions about scaling. Leveraging analytics will enable founders to identify market trends, optimize operations, and enhance customer experiences.

Global Market Expansion: As the world becomes more interconnected, startups will have greater opportunities to expand into international markets. Founders should be prepared to navigate cultural differences, regulatory challenges, and diverse customer needs.

Scaling startups is an art that requires a delicate balance of strategic thinking, innovation, and effective management. Sam Altman's insights and experiences at Y Combinator have underscored the importance of nurturing a strong culture, achieving product-market fit, building scalable operations, and fostering an environment of experimentation. As startups embark on their scaling journeys, they must embrace challenges, adapt to change, and remain committed to their vision.

By understanding the principles of scaling, founders can navigate the complexities of growth and ensure that their startups not only thrive but also contribute meaningfully to the innovation landscape. Ultimately, the art of nurturing innovation during the scaling process will define the success of tomorrow's startups, shaping the future of entrepreneurship for years to come.

High-Stakes Decisions: Funding the Future Titans of Tech

In the ever-evolving landscape of technology startups, securing funding is one of the most critical milestones that founders must navigate. The decisions surrounding funding can significantly influence a startup's trajectory, shaping its growth potential, market position, and ultimately its success or failure. For Sam Altman, a prominent figure in the tech world and the former president of Y Combinator (YC), the process of funding emerging tech companies involves high stakes, requiring a delicate balance of vision, strategy, and timing. This exploration delves into the intricacies of funding decisions, the challenges faced by startups, the different funding avenues available, and the overarching principles that guide the investment landscape.

Importance of Funding in the Technological Ecosystem

Funding plays a pivotal role in the tech ecosystem, serving as the lifeblood for startups striving to innovate and disrupt traditional markets. It enables entrepreneurs to turn their ideas into viable products, scale operations, and capture market share. The availability of funding can accelerate a startup's growth trajectory, allowing it to invest in technology, talent, marketing, and infrastructure.

However, the process of securing funding is often fraught with challenges. Founders must navigate a complex landscape of investors, venture capitalists, and funding options, each with their own expectations and requirements. The stakes are high, as funding decisions can dictate not only the immediate future of a startup but also its long-term viability.

Types of Funding Available to Startups

Startups have access to various funding options, each with its own advantages and disadvantages. Understanding these avenues is crucial for founders seeking to make informed decisions about their financial futures.

Bootstrapping

Bootstrapping involves funding a startup through personal savings, revenue generated by the business, or informal loans from friends and family. This technique gives founders complete control over their organization without diluting ownership.However, bootstrapping may limit the startup's ability to scale quickly, as founders are often constrained by their financial resources.

Angel Investors

Angel investors are individuals who contribute funding to entrepreneurs in return for stock.They often have industry experience and can offer valuable mentorship in addition to financial support. While angel investment can provide a significant boost in early-stage funding, it typically involves giving up a portion of ownership and control.

Venture Capital

Venture capital firms (VCs) invest in high-growth enterprises in return for shares. VC funding is often sought by startups looking to scale rapidly, as it provides substantial financial backing. However, securing VC investment can be competitive, and investors may impose strict conditions, including board representation and operational oversight.

Crowdfunding

Crowdfunding platforms allow startups to raise small amounts of money from a large number of individuals, often through pre-sales of products or equity offerings. This approach democratizes fundraising and provides startups with an opportunity to gauge market interest. However, crowdfunding requires effective marketing and a compelling pitch to attract backers.

Government Grants and Subsidies

Various government programs provide grants and subsidies to support innovation and entrepreneurship. These funds do not require equity and can help startups bridge funding gaps. However, navigating the application process can be time-consuming, and competition for these funds may be high.

The Funding Decision-Making Process

The funding decision-making process involves multiple steps, each of which requires careful consideration and strategic thinking. Altman's experiences at Y Combinator have shed light on the critical elements that entrepreneurs must evaluate when seeking funding.

Assessing Financial Needs

Founders must begin by thoroughly assessing their financial needs. This includes estimating the capital required to develop their product, cover operational expenses, and achieve specific milestones. A well-defined financial plan helps entrepreneurs determine how much funding they need and what type of funding is most suitable for their situation.

2. Evaluating Funding Sources

Once financial needs are established, founders must evaluate potential funding sources. This involves considering the pros and cons of each option, as well as aligning the chosen source with the startup's vision and goals. For instance, if maintaining control is a priority, bootstrapping or seeking angel investment may be more appropriate than pursuing venture capital.

Preparing a Compelling Pitch

A great pitch is essential for attracting interested investors.Founders must clearly articulate their value proposition, market opportunity, business model, and growth strategy. Demonstrating a deep understanding of the industry, competition, and customer needs can help build credibility and instill confidence in potential investors.

Building Relationships with Investors

Funding is not solely about the money; it also involves building relationships with investors. Founders should focus on establishing trust and rapport with potential investors, as strong relationships can lead to valuable mentorship and guidance beyond financial support. Engaging with investors early in the process, even before seeking funding, can help cultivate these relationships.

Negotiating Terms

Once a startup secures interest from investors, the negotiation process begins. Founders must carefully navigate discussions around equity stakes, valuation, board representation, and other terms. Balancing the need for funding with the desire to retain control is crucial during this stage. Founders should seek to understand the implications of their agreements and negotiate terms that align with their long-term vision.

Challenges in Funding Decisions

Navigating the funding landscape comes with its own set of challenges. Entrepreneurs must be prepared to face potential pitfalls that could hinder their progress.

Market Conditions

Market circumstances can have a substantial influence on a startup's ability to raise funds. . Economic downturns or fluctuations in investor sentiment may lead to increased competition for limited funding.

Founders must stay informed about market trends and be adaptable in their funding strategies.

Investor Expectations

Investors often have high expectations regarding growth and returns. Founders must align their vision with investor goals while maintaining their own priorities. Balancing short-term performance metrics with long-term growth strategies is essential to meet investor expectations without compromising the startup's mission.

Dilution of Ownership

Seeking external funding often leads to the dilution of ownership for founders. This can create tension, especially if founders are forced to give up significant control of their company. It's essential for entrepreneurs to carefully weigh the trade-offs associated with funding decisions and seek to minimize dilution while still securing the capital needed for growth.

Maintaining Focus

The pursuit of funding can sometimes distract founders from their core business activities. It's important for entrepreneurs to maintain focus on product development, customer acquisition, and team building, even while navigating the complexities of funding. Founders should allocate time and resources wisely to ensure that they continue to drive their business forward.

The Role of Y Combinator in Funding Startups

At Y Combinator, Altman has witnessed firsthand the transformative power of strategic funding decisions for startups. YC has become a renowned accelerator that provides early-stage companies with not only funding but also mentorship, networking opportunities, and resources to scale successfully.

Seed Funding and Beyond: YC offers seed funding to selected startups, allowing them to focus on developing their ideas without immediate financial pressures. This initial investment often serves as a springboard for subsequent funding rounds as startups gain traction and validation.

Mentorship and Guidance: In addition to finance, YC offers crucial mentorship from seasoned entrepreneurs and investors. Founders benefit from tailored advice on funding strategies, market positioning, and navigating the complexities of growth.

Investor Connections: YC's extensive network of investors opens doors for startups seeking additional funding. The accelerator facilitates introductions to potential investors, enhancing the startup's chances of securing future rounds of financing.

Focus on Product-Market Fit: YC emphasizes the importance of achieving product-market fit before pursuing aggressive scaling. This focus ensures that startups are not only funded but also equipped to sustain growth in the long term.

Looking Ahead: The Future of Funding in Tech

As the tech landscape continues to evolve, so too will the funding strategies and opportunities available to startups. Emerging trends and technologies are likely to reshape the funding ecosystem in several ways.

Decentralized Finance (DeFi): The rise of DeFi platforms offers new avenues for startups to secure funding without traditional intermediaries. Smart contracts and blockchain technology can facilitate transparent funding processes, allowing entrepreneurs to access capital more efficiently.

Impact Investing: Investors increasingly seek to align their capital with social and environmental impact.

Startups that prioritize sustainability and social responsibility may find new funding opportunities through impact investors who share similar values.

Globalization of Funding: The global nature of the tech industry allows startups to tap into international funding sources. As remote work and digital communication become the norm, founders can connect with investors from around the world, broadening their funding possibilities.

Enhanced Data Analytics: The increasing availability of data will empower investors to make more informed funding decisions. Startups that leverage data analytics to demonstrate their market potential, customer engagement, and growth prospects will have a competitive advantage in securing funding.

High-stakes funding decisions are integral to the success of tech startups, shaping their growth potential and market positioning. For Sam Altman, the process of funding future titans of tech involves a careful balance of strategy, relationship-building, and adaptability. By understanding the various funding avenues, evaluating their financial needs, and navigating the complexities of negotiations, founders can position themselves for success.

As the tech landscape evolves, entrepreneurs must remain attuned to emerging trends and opportunities that can enhance their funding strategies. By leveraging resources like Y Combinator and embracing innovative funding approaches, startups can navigate the high-stakes world of funding and emerge as the next generation of industry leaders. Ultimately, the decisions made today will shape the future of technology, enabling innovators to create lasting impact and drive meaningful change in the world.

Empowering a New Generation of Entrepreneurs

In an era marked by rapid technological advancements and an increasingly interconnected global economy, entrepreneurship has emerged as a powerful force for innovation and societal change. As we look to the future, empowering a new generation of entrepreneurs is not only essential for economic growth but also for addressing pressing challenges such as climate change, social inequality, and public health. Sam Altman, as a leading figure in the tech world and former president of Y Combinator, has been at the forefront of fostering entrepreneurial spirit and providing resources to help aspiring founders succeed. This exploration delves into the key factors that empower the next generation of entrepreneurs, the challenges they face, and the role of ecosystems that support entrepreneurial endeavors.

The Importance of Empowering Entrepreneurs

Empowering entrepreneurs is vital for several reasons:

Economic Growth: Startups are a significant driver of job creation and innovation. By empowering entrepreneurs, we can stimulate economic growth, foster competition, and create new industries that contribute to a more robust economy.

Innovation and Disruption: Entrepreneurs are often at the forefront of innovation, developing solutions that challenge the status quo. Empowering them enables the exploration of new ideas, technologies, and business models that can lead to transformative change across various sectors.

Social Impact: Many entrepreneurs are driven by a desire to address social and environmental issues. By empowering individuals to create businesses that prioritize sustainability and social responsibility, we can foster a generation of leaders who are committed to making a positive impact on society.

Diversity of Ideas: Empowering a diverse group of entrepreneurs ensures a broader range of perspectives and ideas. Diversity in entrepreneurship leads to more innovative solutions and products that cater to various communities and needs.

Key Factors in Empowering Entrepreneurs

To empower a new generation of entrepreneurs, several key factors must be addressed:

Access to Education and Resources

Education is foundational to entrepreneurship. Programs that focus on business fundamentals, financial literacy, and innovation can equip aspiring entrepreneurs with the knowledge and skills they need to succeed. This can include:

Entrepreneurial Curriculum: Incorporating entrepreneurship education into schools and universities can inspire students to explore business creation early on. Curriculum focused on practical skills, such as marketing, finance, and product development, can be particularly beneficial.

Workshops and Bootcamps: Short-term programs that offer intensive training and mentorship can provide aspiring entrepreneurs with actionable insights and networking opportunities. These workshops can cover various aspects of launching a business, from ideation to fundraising.

Access to Funding

Securing funding is often one of the most significant hurdles for aspiring entrepreneurs. Creating pathways for access to capital is essential for empowering the next generation. This can be achieved through:

Microfinance and Seed Funding: Initiatives that provide small loans or seed funding to startups can help entrepreneurs take their first steps. Microfinance institutions can play a critical role in supporting those who may lack access to traditional banking systems.

Crowdfunding Platforms: Crowdfunding has democratized access to capital by allowing entrepreneurs to raise funds from the public. Promoting awareness and education around crowdfunding can empower more individuals to explore this avenue.

Venture Capital and Angel Investment: Building networks that connect entrepreneurs with investors can create more opportunities for funding. Investors who are passionate about supporting emerging entrepreneurs can help bridge the funding gap.

Mentorship and Networking Opportunities

Mentorship is a powerful tool for empowering entrepreneurs. Experienced mentors can provide invaluable guidance, advice, and support to help navigate the challenges of starting and scaling a business. Key elements include:

Mentorship Programs: Establishing formal mentorship programs that connect experienced entrepreneurs with newcomers can foster relationships that drive growth and development. These programs can provide mentees with insights into industry best practices, funding strategies, and operational challenges.

Networking Events: Hosting networking events and conferences allows entrepreneurs to connect with peers, investors, and industry experts. Building relationships within the entrepreneurial ecosystem can lead to collaborations, partnerships, and funding opportunities.

Online Communities: In the digital age, online platforms provide avenues for entrepreneurs to share experiences, seek advice, and build connections. Creating inclusive online communities can empower entrepreneurs globally.

Creating Inclusive Entrepreneurial Ecosystems

Building an inclusive entrepreneurial ecosystem is essential for empowering a diverse group of entrepreneurs. This involves:

Supportive Policies: Governments can implement policies that foster entrepreneurship by reducing regulatory barriers, providing tax incentives for startups, and creating incubators and innovation hubs.

Diversity and Inclusion Initiatives: Encouraging diversity in entrepreneurship by supporting underrepresented groups, including women and minorities, can lead to a broader range of ideas and solutions. Initiatives that focus on inclusion and access can help level the playing field.

Collaborative Spaces: Co-working spaces, incubators, and accelerators can provide the infrastructure and resources entrepreneurs need to thrive. These spaces often foster collaboration, innovation, and community building.

Challenges Facing New Entrepreneurs

While there are numerous opportunities for aspiring entrepreneurs, challenges persist that must be addressed to empower them effectively:

Access to Capital: Despite the growth of funding options, many entrepreneurs still struggle to secure financing, particularly those from underrepresented backgrounds. Barriers such as discrimination in lending practices and limited networks can hinder access to capital.

Fear of Failure: The fear of failure can be a significant deterrent for aspiring entrepreneurs. Cultivating a culture that embraces experimentation and views failure as a learning opportunity is essential to empower individuals to take risks.

Market Saturation: In highly competitive markets, standing out can be challenging. Entrepreneurs must navigate crowded spaces and find unique value propositions to capture market share.

Balancing Work and Life: Starting a business requires immense time and dedication. Many entrepreneurs face challenges in balancing their personal and professional lives, leading to burnout and stress.

The Role of Organizations in Empowering Entrepreneurs

Various organizations, including nonprofit organizations, educational institutions, and government agencies, play a vital role in empowering the next generation of entrepreneurs. Initiatives that support entrepreneurship can include:

Incubators and Accelerators: Programs that provide startups with mentorship, resources, and funding opportunities can help accelerate growth and development. These programs often offer structured support to guide entrepreneurs through the early stages of their journey.

Community Development Programs: Local community organizations can create initiatives that promote entrepreneurship, particularly in underserved areas. Programs that provide training, funding, and networking opportunities can empower individuals to start businesses in their communities.

Corporate Social Responsibility Initiatives: Corporations can engage in CSR efforts that support entrepreneurship by providing funding, mentorship, and resources to startups. Partnerships between established companies and startups can foster innovation and create mutually beneficial relationships.

The Future of Entrepreneurship

As we look ahead, the future of entrepreneurship is likely to be shaped by several emerging trends:

Technological Innovation: Advances in technology will continue to open new avenues for entrepreneurship. Fields such as artificial intelligence, biotechnology, and renewable energy present opportunities for entrepreneurs to create disruptive solutions.

Social Entrepreneurship: A growing focus on social impact and sustainability is driving the rise of social entrepreneurship. Entrepreneurs who prioritize social responsibility and environmental sustainability will play a crucial role in addressing global challenges.

Remote Work and Global Markets: The rise of remote work and digital communication has expanded opportunities for entrepreneurs to tap into global markets. Entrepreneurs can now build teams and serve customers from anywhere in the world.

Collaboration Over Competition: The future may see a shift toward collaborative business models, where entrepreneurs work together to solve problems and create value. Cooperative ventures and partnerships can enhance innovation and drive success.

Empowering a new generation of entrepreneurs is essential for fostering innovation, economic growth, and social change. By addressing key factors such as access to education, funding, mentorship, and inclusive ecosystems, we can create an environment that nurtures aspiring entrepreneurs.

As Sam Altman and others continue to champion entrepreneurship through initiatives like Y Combinator, the focus remains on building a supportive infrastructure that empowers diverse voices and ideas. By investing in the next generation of entrepreneurs, we can unlock their potential to drive meaningful change and create a brighter, more innovative future for all.

CHAPTER 3: STEPPING UP AS A VISIONARY LEADER – THE OPENAI JOURNEY BEGINS

Understanding the AI Opportunity

Artificial Intelligence (AI) has rapidly evolved from a futuristic concept into a transformative technology with profound implications across industries, societies, and economies. The AI opportunity encompasses a wide range of applications, from automating mundane tasks and enhancing business processes to revolutionizing healthcare and addressing complex global challenges. As AI continues to advance, it presents immense potential for innovation, economic growth, and social impact. Understanding this opportunity involves exploring AI's current capabilities, its potential applications, the challenges it presents, and the steps required to harness its benefits responsibly.

The Evolution of AI and Its Present Capabilities

AI encompasses a variety of technologies, including machine learning (ML), natural language processing

(NLP), computer vision, robotics, and neural networks. Several significant milestones have shaped its evolution: Early Development (1950s–1980s): The term "artificial intelligence" was first coined in the 1950s, with early research focused on symbolic reasoning, problem-solving, and basic algorithms. These initial efforts laid the groundwork for later advancements but were limited by computing power and data availability.

Machine Learning Breakthroughs (1990s–2000s): The rise of machine learning, which enables computers to learn from data rather than relying on hard-coded rules, marked a significant shift. Algorithms like decision trees, support vector machines, and neural networks gained popularity, setting the stage for deep learning.

Deep Learning and Big Data (2010s–Present): The proliferation of big data and advancements in computational power have propelled deep learning, a subset of machine learning that uses artificial neural networks to model complex patterns. This breakthrough enabled significant progress in image recognition, speech processing, and language translation.

Generative AI and Transformers (2020s): More recently, the development of generative AI models, such as OpenAI's GPT (Generative Pre-trained Transformer), has opened new possibilities in content creation, automated coding, and conversational interfaces. Transformers, a type of deep learning model, excel at understanding context in sequences of data, making them highly effective for tasks like NLP.

Key Areas Where AI Is Transforming Industries

The AI opportunity is evident across multiple sectors, with applications reshaping everything from business operations to scientific research. Some of the most important areas of influence are:

Healthcare

AI is revolutionizing healthcare by improving diagnostics, personalized medicine, and patient outcomes. Key applications include:

Medical Imaging: AI-powered algorithms can analyze medical images such as X-rays, MRIs, and CT scans with high accuracy, detecting anomalies and diseases like cancer earlier than traditional methods.

Drug Discovery: Machine learning models are used to predict the effectiveness of new compounds, accelerating the drug discovery process. This reduces the time and cost associated with bringing new medicines to market.

Personalized Treatment: AI can analyze genetic data, medical history, and lifestyle factors to recommend personalized treatment plans. Predictive models can also forecast patient outcomes, helping clinicians make more informed decisions.

Finance

In the financial sector, AI improves decision-making, risk management, and customer service:

Algorithmic Trading: AI models can analyze large datasets to identify trading patterns and execute trades at optimal times, increasing profitability for investment firms.

Fraud Detection: Machine learning algorithms are adept at detecting anomalies in transaction data, flagging potential fraud, and preventing financial crimes.

Chatbots and Customer Service: AI-driven chatbots provide instant customer support, handle routine inquiries, and assist with financial planning, improving the customer experience.

Manufacturing and Supply Chain

AI is driving efficiency and innovation in manufacturing processes and supply chain management:

Predictive Maintenance: AI systems can anticipate equipment breakdowns, lowering downtime and maintenance expenses. Sensors and AI-powered analytics monitor machinery for signs of wear and tear, allowing for proactive maintenance.

Quality Control: Computer vision systems use AI to inspect products for defects, ensuring consistent quality and reducing waste.

Supply Chain Optimization: AI algorithms help optimize inventory levels, forecast demand, and streamline logistics, leading to cost savings and improved supply chain resilience.

Transportation and Autonomous Vehicles

The transportation industry is witnessing a significant shift with the integration of AI in autonomous driving, logistics, and traffic management:

Self-Driving Cars: AI-powered systems use sensors, cameras, and deep learning models to navigate roads, recognize obstacles, and make real-time driving decisions. Companies like Tesla, Waymo, and others are advancing autonomous vehicle technology.

Logistics Automation: AI optimizes delivery routes, fleet management, and warehouse operations, making logistics more efficient and cost-effective.

Traffic Prediction and Management: AI can analyze traffic patterns and predict congestion, allowing city planners to optimize traffic flow and reduce travel times.

5. Retail and E-commerce

AI is transforming the retail business by improving consumer experiences, managing inventories, and increasing revenues.

Personalized Recommendations: E-commerce platforms use AI to analyze browsing and purchase histories, offering personalized product recommendations to customers, thereby increasing conversion rates.

Dynamic Pricing: Machine learning models can adjust prices in real-time based on demand, competition, and other factors to maximize revenue.

Inventory Management: AI-driven analytics predict which products are likely to sell, enabling retailers to optimize stock levels and reduce overstock or stockouts.

Emerging AI Applications

The AI landscape continues to evolve, and new applications are emerging that could reshape industries further:

Generative AI in Content Creation: Tools like GPT-3, DALL-E, and Stable Diffusion allow for the generation of high-quality text, images, and audio. These applications extend to marketing content, code generation, design, and even entertainment, automating creative tasks.

AI in Education: Personalized learning platforms powered by AI can adapt to students' individual needs, providing tailored content and feedback. AI can also help to automate administrative operations like grading and scheduling.

AI for Environmental Sustainability: AI-driven models can optimize energy consumption, improve resource management, and monitor environmental changes. For example, AI can enhance weather forecasting accuracy, support conservation efforts, and optimize agriculture for better yields with lower environmental impact.

Challenges and Risks Associated with AI

While AI presents substantial opportunities, it also poses significant challenges and risks that need to be addressed:

Ethical Concerns

The ethical implications of AI are a major concern, particularly regarding privacy, bias, and the potential for misuse:

Bias in AI Models: AI systems can inherit biases from the data they are trained on, resulting in unfair or discriminating conclusions. This can be problematic in areas such as hiring, law enforcement, and lending.

Privacy Issues: AI's ability to process vast amounts of personal data raises privacy concerns. The use of AI for surveillance or data mining must be balanced with the need to protect individual rights.

Autonomous Weapons: The use of AI in military applications, such as autonomous weapons systems, raises ethical questions about the potential for unintended consequences and loss of human oversight.

Economic Disruption

AI's impact on the job market is a double-edged sword, potentially leading to economic disruption:

Job Displacement: Automation powered by AI could displace workers in industries such as manufacturing, logistics, and retail. While new job opportunities may arise, there may be a skills gap that leaves some workers behind.

Economic Inequality: The benefits of AI may be unevenly distributed, with large technology companies and skilled workers reaping most of the rewards. Policymakers must consider how to mitigate inequality and ensure broader access to AI's advantages.

Security and Safety

As AI systems are increasingly incorporated into key infrastructure, it is important to ensure their security and safety.

Adversarial Attacks: AI models can be vulnerable to adversarial attacks, which alter inputs to create inaccurate results. This can be particularly dangerous in areas like autonomous driving or healthcare.

Reliability and Accountability: Determining who is accountable when AI systems fail can be challenging. Ensuring that AI models are reliable, interpretable, and transparent is essential for their safe deployment.

Strategies for Maximizing the AI Opportunity

To fully harness the AI opportunity, several strategies need to be adopted by businesses, governments, and society at large:

Investing in Research and Development: Continued investment in AI research is crucial for advancing the technology. Governments, universities, and private companies should collaborate to drive innovation and solve pressing challenges in AI.

Fostering a Skilled Workforce: Preparing the workforce for an AI-driven future is essential. This includes promoting STEM education, offering training programs in AI and data science, and upskilling workers whose jobs may be affected by automation.

Implementing Ethical AI Guidelines: Organizations should adopt ethical guidelines for AI development to ensure that models are fair, transparent, and accountable. Addressing issues like bias, privacy, and security proactively will help build public trust in AI systems.

Encouraging Public-Private Partnerships: Collaboration between governments and private companies can accelerate AI adoption while ensuring that regulations keep pace with technological advancements. Public-private partnerships can also help in funding AI initiatives that benefit society, such as healthcare and environmental projects.

Promoting AI for Social Good: AI should be leveraged to address global challenges such as poverty, climate change, and disease prevention. By focusing on AI applications that have a positive social impact, we can ensure that technology benefits all of humanity.

The Role of Visionaries like Sam Altman

Visionary leaders like Sam Altman play a critical role in shaping the future of AI by supporting innovative startups, guiding ethical AI development, and advocating for responsible use of technology. During his tenure at Y Combinator, Altman backed numerous AI-focused startups, fostering an environment where experimentation and cutting-edge research could thrive. His involvement with OpenAI further underscores his commitment to AI's transformative potential, aiming to develop artificial general intelligence (AGI) that is safe, fair, and aligned with human values.

Understanding the AI opportunity requires not only a recognition of its potential to revolutionize industries but also a commitment to addressing its challenges responsibly. With advancements in healthcare, finance, manufacturing, and beyond, AI presents enormous prospects for growth and innovation. However, ethical considerations, economic disruption, and security risks must be managed to realize AI's benefits equitably. As leaders, policymakers, and society navigate this evolving landscape, the focus should remain on using AI to drive positive change while ensuring that technology serves humanity as a whole.

The Founding Vision of OpenAI: Ethics and Advancement

The founding of OpenAI marked a pivotal moment in the development of artificial intelligence (AI), establishing an organization dedicated to the ethical advancement of AI technology for the benefit of humanity. Founded in 2015 by Sam Altman, Elon Musk,

Greg Brockman, Ilya Sutskever, John Schulman, and Wojciech Zaremba, OpenAI's mission is rooted in the belief that artificial general intelligence (AGI)—an AI system with intelligence comparable to that of a human—should be developed in a way that is safe, transparent, and aligned with human values. The organization set out to ensure that AGI, once created, would be a tool that enhances human potential and addresses global challenges, rather than posing risks to society.

The Inspiration Behind OpenAI's Founding

The vision for OpenAI emerged from a combination of factors, including:

The Rapid Pace of AI Development: The mid-2010s saw significant breakthroughs in AI, particularly in machine learning and deep learning. These advances made it clear that AI was on a trajectory toward increasingly sophisticated capabilities, raising questions about its future impact on society.

The Potential Risks of Uncontrolled AGI: As AI researchers progressed toward AGI, concerns arose about its potential dangers. Uncontrolled or malicious use of AGI could lead to outcomes such as economic disruption, authoritarian surveillance, or even existential risks if the technology were to act in ways detrimental to humanity.

Ensuring Broad Access to AI's Benefits: There was a growing recognition that if AI technology remained in the hands of a few corporations or governments, it could exacerbate existing inequalities. The founders of OpenAI aimed to democratize AI, making its benefits accessible to everyone while ensuring that the technology's development remained accountable.

Ethical Concerns About AI Use: Ethical issues, including privacy violations, biased algorithms, and job displacement due to automation, were becoming more pronounced. OpenAI was founded on the principle that AI should be used ethically, with safeguards in place to address these concerns proactively.

OpenAI's Core Principles and Mission

OpenAI was established with a mission to ensure that artificial general intelligence (AGI) benefits all of humanity. Its core principles have guided its approach to AI development:

Broadly Distributed Benefits: OpenAI's mission emphasizes that AGI's benefits should be shared widely, rather than concentrated in the hands of a few. The organization is committed to ensuring that AGI, when developed, helps solve humanity's biggest challenges, such as poverty, disease, and climate change.

Long-Term Safety: Ensuring the safety of AGI is a primary concern. OpenAI is dedicated to conducting research to make AGI safe and to developing strategies to address risks associated with AGI deployment. This includes building mechanisms to prevent harmful uses of AI and creating systems that can align AGI behavior with human values.

Technical Leadership: OpenAI aims to be at the forefront of AI research and development, advancing the state of the art in AI capabilities. By leading technical progress, the organization seeks to shape the trajectory of AI development in ways that prioritize safety and ethical considerations.

Cooperation: OpenAI actively collaborates with other research and policy institutions to share its insights and engage in discussions on AI safety and ethics. This cooperative approach extends to promoting the responsible governance of AI at an international level.

Avoiding AI Arms Race Dynamics: The founders were concerned about the possibility of an AI arms race, where competing entities might rush to develop AGI without proper safety measures. OpenAI advocates for cooperation between AI developers to prevent this scenario and ensure that safety standards are upheld.

OpenAI's Unique Approach to Research and Ethics

OpenAI's research and development approach reflects its commitment to balancing technological advancement with ethical considerations:

Transparency and Openness

OpenAI's name reflects its foundational commitment to openness. The organization initially embraced a policy of publishing research papers, sharing software, and releasing data to the broader AI community. This approach aimed to foster collaboration and accelerate scientific progress by making cutting-edge AI research accessible.

However, the challenge of balancing openness with safety became evident with the development of powerful language models like GPT-2 and GPT-3. OpenAI chose not to release GPT-2 fully at first, citing concerns that it could be used for harmful purposes such as generating fake news or malicious content. This decision marked a shift toward "staged release," where research findings are shared gradually to ensure responsible use.

Focus on AI Alignment and Safety

One of OpenAI's key research areas is AI alignment—the process of ensuring that AI systems understand and adhere to human values. This includes developing techniques for aligning the behavior of AI models with the intentions and ethical norms of their human operators. Research in AI safety encompasses:

Reinforcement Learning from Human Feedback (RLHF):

This technique involves training AI models using feedback from human evaluators to improve their performance and align their behavior with human preferences.

Robustness and Interpretability: OpenAI invests in making AI models more interpretable and robust, meaning they can be better understood and are more resistant to adversarial manipulation.

Mitigating Bias: AI models can inherit biases present in their training data. OpenAI works to identify and reduce bias in its models, ensuring fairer and more equitable outcomes.

Development of Safe AGI

While current AI models like GPT-4 are not AGI, OpenAI is actively preparing for the development of AGI. The organization conducts research on safety frameworks, containment mechanisms, and governance structures that will be necessary when AGI-level systems emerge. This includes strategies for:

Controlled Deployment: OpenAI aims to ensure that AGI systems are deployed in a controlled and incremental manner, with continuous monitoring for safety and ethical impacts.

Collaborative Development: The organization seeks to involve other stakeholders, including governments, academic institutions, and industry leaders, in the development and oversight of AGI to ensure that its deployment is collectively governed.

The Evolution of OpenAI's Organizational Structure

OpenAI began as a non-profit research organization with a mission to advance digital intelligence in a way that benefits humanity. However, in 2019, the organization transitioned to a "capped-profit" model, creating OpenAI LP, a for-profit entity with a unique structure designed to balance profit incentives with its mission-driven goals. Key aspects of this structure include:

Capped Returns for Investors: Investors in OpenAI LP can earn a return on their investment, but the profits are capped at a predetermined level. This approach is intended to attract funding for AI research while ensuring that the bulk of any future profits are used to support OpenAI's mission.

Non-Profit Oversight: OpenAI's board of directors, which oversees the organization's activities, remains part of the original non-profit entity. The board is responsible for ensuring that OpenAI LP's activities align with the overarching mission to benefit humanity.

Ethical Dilemmas and OpenAI's Response

As AI capabilities advance, ethical dilemmas have arisen, prompting OpenAI to navigate complex issues related to safety, privacy, and societal impact:

Concerns Over Misinformation and Deepfakes

Language models like GPT-3 and GPT-4 are capable of generating highly convincing text, raising concerns about their potential misuse to spread misinformation, generate deepfake content, or conduct phishing attacks..

OpenAI has addressed these issues by:

Implementing Use-Case Restrictions: OpenAI's API terms of service prohibit using its models for illegal activities, disinformation, and other harmful purposes.

Content Moderation Tools: The organization has developed and integrated content moderation tools to help users filter and prevent the generation of harmful or unethical outputs.

Navigating Corporate Partnerships and Revenue Models

OpenAI's partnerships with companies like Microsoft, which invested $1 billion in 2019 and collaborated on integrating OpenAI's models with Azure, have sparked debates about the balance between commercial interests and the organization's ethical mission. To address these concerns:

Ethical Guardrails in Partnerships: OpenAI works with partners who share its commitment to ethical AI development. The organization ensures that commercial applications of its technology adhere to ethical standards.

Continued Commitment to Research Transparency: Despite increasing commercialization, OpenAI continues to publish research findings and promote transparency in its work to foster collaboration within the AI research community.

OpenAI's Long-Term Vision: AGI and Its Implications

The long-term vision of OpenAI extends beyond creating advanced AI models to the development of AGI. The organization's approach to AGI is characterized by:

Ensuring AGI Benefits Everyone: OpenAI's mission explicitly states that AGI should work to benefit all of humanity. This goal involves taking proactive steps to avoid scenarios where AGI's benefits are disproportionately controlled by a small group or used in ways that harm society.

Global Cooperation: OpenAI recognizes that the development of AGI will be a global endeavor requiring international cooperation. The organization supports the establishment of global norms and policies for AGI governance to ensure that all nations can benefit from and contribute to AGI development.

Ethical Development and Deployment: OpenAI is committed to developing AGI safely and responsibly. This includes conducting risk assessments, engaging in safety research, and adopting deployment strategies that emphasize incremental progress and alignment with human values.

The Role of Sam Altman in Shaping OpenAI's Mission

As a co-founder and current CEO of OpenAI, Sam Altman has played a crucial role in shaping the organization's mission and ethical stance. His leadership is characterized by:

Advocacy for Ethical AI Development: Altman has consistently emphasized the need for AI to be developed with safety and ethical considerations at the forefront. His public statements and strategic decisions reflect a commitment to ensuring AI benefits society as a whole.

Promoting Collaboration Across the AI Community: Altman supports OpenAI's cooperative approach, advocating for collaboration with other AI research organizations and policymakers to collectively address safety and ethical challenges.

Balancing Innovation with Responsibility: Under Altman's leadership, OpenAI has pursued a path that balances cutting-edge AI research with a cautious approach to deployment, especially concerning models that have the potential to significantly impact society.

The founding vision of OpenAI reflects a commitment to advancing AI in a way that prioritizes ethics, safety, and the common good. By establishing core principles focused on broadly distributed benefits, long-term safety, and transparency, OpenAI aims to shape the future of AI in ways that maximize its positive impact while addressing potential risks. The organization's evolution, including its shift to a capped-profit model and strategic partnerships, demonstrates a flexible approach to navigating ethical challenges without compromising its mission. As OpenAI continues to pursue the development of AGI, its founding vision will guide efforts to ensure that this transformative technology remains aligned with human values and benefits all of humanity.

Leading the Charge: From Idea to Execution

Sam Altman's journey in the tech world is defined by his ability to transform bold ideas into impactful reality. Throughout his career, he has demonstrated an uncanny ability to recognize promising opportunities, build teams, and drive innovations that have had lasting effects across various sectors. His leadership style—centered on execution, strategic vision, and an unyielding focus on problem-solving—has enabled him to shape the course of startups and tech companies alike. This chapter delves into how Altman has led the charge in translating innovative concepts into executed strategies, highlighting key examples of his approach.

Early Influences on Altman's Leadership Style

Altman's inclination towards hands-on leadership and execution stems from his early experiences in the tech startup environment. Founding the social location-based service, Loopt, while still in college, he quickly learned the importance of turning an idea into a functional product. Loopt may not have achieved massive commercial success, but it provided valuable lessons in perseverance, market timing, and adapting to user needs. These experiences became fundamental to his approach in later endeavors.

The knowledge gained from Loopt served Altman well when he took the helm at Y Combinator (YC), where he was able to influence the trajectories of countless startups directly. As a key player at YC, he helped hundreds of founders navigate the difficult journey from idea to execution, guiding funding, product development, and scaling. His time at YC honed his skills in identifying potential and nurturing it to fruition, which would prove critical in his later role at OpenAI.

The Y Combinator Approach: Nurturing Startups from Concept to Product

When Altman became the president of Y Combinator in 2014, he brought with him a clear vision for scaling the startup accelerator's impact. Under his leadership, YC expanded its reach by funding a more diverse array of startups, including those pursuing ambitious technological goals with longer timelines for development. Altman's strategic shift allowed YC to broaden its scope, enabling not only the traditional software startups but also hardware companies, biotech firms, and even projects focused on nuclear fusion and space exploration.

He believed in fostering a culture of rapid experimentation and iteration, advising founders to launch products quickly and gather user feedback, rather than aiming for perfection in early versions. This "launch fast and iterate" philosophy became a hallmark of YC's approach under Altman's leadership, and it was instrumental in enabling startups to evolve their ideas based on real-world feedback. Companies such as Airbnb, Dropbox, and Reddit benefitted from this culture of rapid execution and strategic growth nurtured during their time at YC.

Altman emphasized the importance of founders staying deeply involved in the execution phase, especially in the early stages of their startups. He often advocated for founders to immerse themselves in understanding the needs of their first users, enabling them to refine their products in a way that truly resonated with the market. This hands-on approach was not just about iterating products; it was about building a company culture that prioritized execution, resilience, and adaptability.

Strategic Execution in OpenAI: Scaling AI Research from Idea to Impact

Taking the helm at OpenAI marked a new chapter for Altman, where the challenge wasn't just about nurturing individual startups but leading a groundbreaking research initiative aimed at advancing artificial general intelligence (AGI). OpenAI's mission to ensure that AGI benefits all of humanity required not only a vision but also a detailed execution plan involving large-scale research and complex technical projects.

Altman approached the task of scaling AI research by focusing on three key pillars: setting ambitious goals, securing necessary resources, and fostering a culture of ethical innovation.

Setting Ambitious, Yet Realistic Goals

At OpenAI, Altman played a central role in establishing ambitious goals that were both inspiring and technically feasible. He encouraged the team to work on projects with significant societal impact, such as natural language processing models, robotics, and reinforcement learning. By setting clear, outcome-oriented goals—like developing powerful language models (e.g., GPT series)—Altman enabled OpenAI to push the boundaries of what was possible in AI research while maintaining a commitment to safety and ethical considerations.

A critical aspect of Altman's leadership in goal-setting was his insistence on long-term thinking. He understood that meaningful advancements in AI would not happen overnight, and that achieving AGI would involve a series of intermediate milestones. This mindset helped OpenAI to focus not just on short-term accomplishments but on sustained, incremental progress that would eventually lead to transformative outcomes.

Securing Resources and Strategic Partnerships

Another vital component of leading the charge at OpenAI involved securing the resources necessary to achieve the organization's ambitious goals. Altman recognized early on that the computational demands of cutting-edge AI research would require significant funding and infrastructure. In 2019, OpenAI formed a landmark partnership with Microsoft, securing a $1 billion investment. This strategic alliance provided

OpenAI with access to Microsoft's cloud computing platform, Azure, enabling it to scale its experiments and models far beyond what had previously been possible. Altman's ability to secure strategic partnerships and funding reflected his execution-focused approach. Rather than viewing resource limitations as a barrier, he sought out creative solutions to align the interests of key stakeholders, thereby expanding OpenAI's capabilities. The partnership with Microsoft not only provided financial support but also signaled a shift in how AI research could be funded and managed, blending the advantages of both corporate and research-focused organizations.

Fostering a Culture of Ethical Innovation

At the heart of OpenAI's mission is the commitment to ethical AI development, and Altman has been a driving force behind fostering a culture where ethics are not an afterthought but a guiding principle. He has consistently highlighted the importance of considering the societal implications of AI research and has supported initiatives aimed at addressing challenges such as algorithmic bias, data privacy, and the potential misuse of AI technology.

One notable example of Altman's leadership in this area is OpenAI's approach to releasing new technologies. For instance, when OpenAI developed the GPT-2 language model, it initially withheld the full release due to concerns about its potential misuse for generating misinformation or malicious content. This decision reflected a cautious approach to execution, prioritizing ethical considerations over the immediate impact of releasing cutting-edge technology.

Overcoming Challenges and Learning from Failures

Executing ambitious ideas in the realm of startups and AI research is not without its setbacks, and Altman's journey includes learning from failures as much as from successes. His experiences have underscored the importance of adaptability and resilience in leadership.

Navigating Market Dynamics and Timing

Timing is often critical in determining whether a new technology will succeed or fail. Altman learned this firsthand with Loopt, where the concept of location-based social networking was ahead of its time. Despite having an innovative idea and securing funding, the market was not ready for widespread adoption. The company eventually struggled against competitors that later emerged with refined approaches. Altman has since emphasized the importance of timing in execution, advising founders to be aware of market readiness and user behavior when launching new products.

Balancing Innovation with Practicality

One of the common challenges faced by innovators is balancing cutting-edge development with practical, user-friendly solutions. At OpenAI, Altman had to navigate this balance, particularly when dealing with the development of large-scale AI models. He led efforts to ensure that the organization did not just focus on developing powerful algorithms but also made these tools accessible and practical for real-world applications.

For example, while creating advanced AI models like GPT-3 and GPT-4, there was a simultaneous effort to provide tools and platforms that enabled developers to integrate AI into their applications easily. This pragmatic approach ensured that OpenAI's innovations were not merely theoretical but could have a tangible impact on industries ranging from healthcare to finance.

Transforming Execution into a Scalable Process

One of Altman's most significant contributions to the field of technology leadership is his ability to transform the process of execution into a scalable model. This is evident in how Y Combinator expanded under his leadership and how OpenAI has structured its approach to research and product development.

Creating a Scalable Framework at Y Combinator

Altman's tenure at YC saw the introduction of programs like YC Continuity, which provided follow-on funding to companies that had previously graduated from the accelerator. This initiative extended YC's support beyond the early startup phase, offering mentorship and resources as companies scale. The idea was to institutionalize a process where startups could receive continuous support from the ideation stage to becoming mature companies.

Implementing Scalable Research Practices at OpenAI

At OpenAI, the scale of research efforts necessitated an approach that could handle vast computational resources and data. Altman's execution strategy included leveraging partnerships for resources and structuring the research teams in ways that encouraged cross-collaboration and open sharing of findings. By implementing scalable research practices, OpenAI could accelerate progress across multiple AI domains simultaneously, ensuring that breakthroughs in one area could inform and enhance efforts in others.

Leading the charge from idea to execution requires more than just vision; it demands a robust strategy, the ability to secure resources, and a commitment to ethical and sustainable growth. Sam Altman's career illustrates these qualities in action, from his early days at Loopt, through his transformative leadership at Y Combinator, to his current role at OpenAI. His execution-focused approach has enabled him to not only drive innovation but also create frameworks that make execution itself a repeatable, scalable process.

Altman's journey is a testament to the power of turning ambitious ideas into reality by addressing challenges and adapting to changing circumstances. Through his leadership, he has shaped companies and influenced the broader technological landscape, laying the groundwork for future innovators to follow.

Navigating the Complexities of AI Development

The development of artificial intelligence (AI) is a multifaceted endeavor that involves tackling numerous technical, ethical, and strategic challenges. As AI progresses towards more advanced capabilities, the complexities associated with building and deploying these systems become increasingly apparent. In his leadership roles at Y Combinator and OpenAI, Sam Altman has had to navigate these complexities, balancing innovation with responsible development and addressing safety, ethics, and societal impact concerns. This chapter explores the various dimensions of AI development, including technical challenges, ethical dilemmas, regulatory considerations, and strategic decision-making, all of which are crucial in shaping the future of AI.

The Technical Complexities of AI Development

Building advanced AI systems like large-scale language models or reinforcement learning agents involves solving various technical problems. These include developing algorithms that can process vast amounts of data, improving the efficiency of training models, and optimizing AI performance to ensure accuracy and reliability.

Data Quality and Quantity

One of the foundational requirements for developing AI is the availability of large and high-quality datasets. The performance of machine learning models, particularly deep learning models, is directly linked to the quality and quantity of the data they are trained on. Ensuring that training data is comprehensive, diverse, and representative of real-world scenarios is a significant challenge.

Data-related complexities include:

Data Bias: If the data used to train AI models is biased, the resulting AI system may exhibit biased behavior, leading to discriminatory outcomes in areas such as hiring, law enforcement, or healthcare.

Data Privacy: Training AI models often involves collecting and using sensitive personal data. Developers must navigate the complexities of data privacy regulations, such as the General Data Protection Regulation (GDPR) in Europe, and implement safeguards to protect users' information.

To address these challenges, AI development teams must prioritize ethical data collection practices, use techniques to mitigate bias, and explore privacy-preserving machine learning methods, such as federated learning and differential privacy.

Algorithm Design and Model Architecture

Choosing the right algorithms and designing effective model architectures are critical steps in AI development. Different tasks, such as natural language processing, computer vision, or game-playing, may require distinct approaches to algorithm selection and model training. For instance, the architecture used in language models, like the transformer architecture that powers GPT-3 and GPT-4, is particularly well-suited for processing sequential data. At the same time, convolutional neural networks excel in image recognition tasks.

Model design considerations include:

Scalability: The ability of an AI model to scale up in terms of data processing and computational power is crucial for tackling large, real-world problems.

Robustness: AI models must be resilient to adversarial inputs, such as images or text, designed to fool the system into making incorrect predictions. Ensuring robustness is an ongoing challenge, especially as models become more complex.

Efficiency: Training large AI models requires substantial computational resources, often resulting in significant energy consumption. Optimizing model training for efficiency is essential for reducing costs and environmental impact.

Altman and his team at OpenAI have continuously worked on refining AI algorithms to address these technical complexities. This includes optimizing training processes to reduce computational demands, designing models more resistant to manipulation, and developing tools that help researchers better understand how AI models make decisions.

The Ethical and Social Complexities of AI

The advancement of AI technology brings about a host of ethical concerns that go beyond the technical realm. AI developers and leaders must confront these issues to ensure that AI systems are used responsibly and do not exacerbate societal problems or create new risks.

Addressing Algorithmic Bias

Algorithmic bias occurs when AI models produce results that unfairly favor certain groups or outcomes due to biased training data. This issue is particularly problematic in facial recognition, lending, hiring, and criminal justice applications, where biased AI decisions can have real-world consequences. Addressing bias requires:

Diverse and Representative Training Data: Efforts must be made to collect data that accurately reflects the real world's diversity. Underrepresentation in data can lead to models that perform well for some groups but poorly for others.

Algorithmic Fairness Techniques: Developers can reduce bias by using methods such as re-weighting training data, adversarial debiasing, and fairness-aware machine learning. However, these techniques are not foolproof and may introduce trade-offs between fairness and model accuracy.

At OpenAI, Sam Altman has advocated for acknowledging and addressing bias in AI systems. The organization prioritizes research into algorithmic fairness and collaborates with other institutions to establish best practices for ethical AI development.

Privacy Concerns and Data Protection

The development of AI often involves handling vast amounts of personal data, which raises significant privacy concerns. Ensuring that AI systems do not infringe on individuals' privacy requires:

Data Anonymization: Techniques such as data anonymization, encryption, and secure multi-party computation can help protect sensitive information during AI training.

Compliance with Privacy Regulations: Organizations like OpenAI must comply with data protection laws, such as the GDPR and the California Consumer Privacy Act (CCPA). This compliance requires implementing data governance policies that safeguard user privacy while still enabling the use of data for AI development.

OpenAI's approach to privacy includes using methods to limit data retention, anonymize training datasets where possible, and develop models that can function effectively without needing access to sensitive data.

The Potential for AI Misuse

As AI models become more capable, concerns about their potential misuse grow. Misuse scenarios include:

Deepfakes: AI can be used to create realistic fake images, videos, or audio recordings, which can spread misinformation or be used for malicious purposes.

Automated Misinformation: Language models can generate convincing fake news articles, posing a risk to information integrity in the digital age.

Weaponization of AI: There is the potential for AI to be used in autonomous weapons or cyber-attacks, raising concerns about military applications and security.

To navigate these ethical complexities, OpenAI has adopted a cautious approach to releasing its technology. For example, when GPT-2 was developed, the organization initially withheld the full release due to concerns about its potential misuse for spreading disinformation. OpenAI later implemented a staged release strategy, gradually providing access to more advanced models while developing guidelines for responsible use.

Strategic and Regulatory Complexities

Navigating AI development also involves making strategic decisions about research priorities, commercial applications, and compliance with emerging regulations.

Balancing Openness and Safety

OpenAI was founded on the principle of openness, aiming to share its research findings and technological advancements with the broader community. However, as the capabilities of its models have grown, so too have concerns about the risks of openly releasing powerful AI technology. This has resulted in a sophisticated approach.

Staged Release of AI Models: Instead of fully releasing new AI models immediately, OpenAI employs a staged approach, gradually increasing access while monitoring for potential misuse.

Publishing Safety Research: OpenAI remains committed to publishing research on AI safety, including work on understanding model behaviors, addressing biases, and ensuring that AI outputs align with user intentions.

This strategy helps balance the benefits of open research with the need for responsible AI deployment, ensuring that advancements do not outpace safety measures.

Engaging with Policymakers and Setting AI Governance Standards

As AI technology continues to evolve, so does the regulatory landscape. Governments and international bodies are increasingly focused on establishing rules for AI use in areas like data privacy, automated decision-making, and the ethical deployment of AI in critical sectors such as healthcare and law enforcement.

Altman and OpenAI have actively engaged with policymakers to shape AI governance standards that prioritize safety and ethical considerations. This engagement includes:

Participating in AI Policy Discussions: OpenAI contributes to conversations on AI policy, offering insights into the potential impacts of AI on society and advising on the creation of regulatory frameworks that address AI safety and ethical concerns.

Advocating for Global Cooperation: Altman has emphasized the need for international cooperation in AI governance to prevent an AI arms race and ensure that AI benefits are distributed equitably.

OpenAI's proactive approach to regulatory engagement reflects its understanding that responsible AI development extends beyond technology—it requires shaping policies that support ethical and safe AI use.

The Organizational Complexities of Scaling AI Research

Scaling AI research involves managing large teams of scientists, securing computational resources, and setting research priorities that align with long-term goals.

1. Building and Leading Multidisciplinary Teams

AI research demands expertise in various fields, including machine learning, computer science, ethics, and policy. Leading such diverse teams involves:

Fostering a Collaborative Culture: OpenAI encourages cross-disciplinary collaboration to integrate different perspectives and expertise into AI development. This helps address the complex challenges associated with AI by combining technical solutions with ethical considerations.

Investing in Talent Development: Attracting and retaining top talent is essential for maintaining a competitive edge in AI research. OpenAI focuses on creating an environment where researchers can work on cutting-edge projects and contribute to high-impact initiatives.

Altman's leadership style at OpenAI emphasizes empowering researchers while setting ambitious goals that drive the organization forward. This approach has enabled OpenAI to tackle some of the most complex problems in AI.

2. Securing Computational Resources

Developing large-scale AI models requires immense computational power. Managing these resources involves strategic decisions about:

Infrastructure Investment: Partnerships, such as the collaboration with Microsoft, provide access to cloud computing infrastructure (Azure), enabling OpenAI to conduct large-scale experiments.

Resource Allocation: OpenAI prioritizes the use of its computational resources for projects that align with its mission, such as advancing safety research and developing models that can solve pressing societal problems.

By securing and effectively managing computational resources, OpenAI ensures that its research efforts are scalable and capable of producing significant advancements in AI.

Managing the Risks of AGI Development

The development of artificial general intelligence (AGI) presents unique challenges, given its potential to fundamentally transform society. Navigating AGI development requires addressing risks related to safety, alignment, and the control of AI systems.

1. Ensuring Safety and Alignment

AGI, which would possess capabilities at or above human level across a wide range of tasks, poses significant safety risks if its goals are not aligned with human values. To address this:

Research on Alignment Techniques: OpenAI focuses on developing methods for aligning AI models with human intentions, such as reinforcement learning from human feedback (RLHF).

Safety Protocols: The organization has established safety protocols that guide how new capabilities are tested and integrated into existing models. This includes conducting extensive red-teaming exercises, where potential risks are identified and mitigated before new AI models are released.

2. Governance Challenges and Long-Term Considerations

Developing AGI is not just a technical endeavor; it also involves establishing governance structures that ensure its development benefits humanity. Key considerations include:

Setting Global Standards: Altman has advocated for international agreements on AGI development to prevent an AI arms race and to ensure safe, collaborative progress.

Preparing for Long-Term Impacts: OpenAI's commitment to AGI development includes preparing for the social and economic implications, such as potential changes in labor markets and the need for robust safety mechanisms.

Navigating the complexities of AI development involves addressing a range of technical, ethical, strategic, and regulatory challenges. Sam Altman's leadership at OpenAI demonstrates a commitment to advancing AI in a manner that prioritizes safety, ethics, and long-term societal benefits. By fostering a culture of ethical innovation, engaging with policymakers, and implementing scalable research practices, Altman and his team at OpenAI are not only pushing the boundaries of what AI can achieve but also setting standards for how it should be developed responsibly. This comprehensive approach to navigating AI's complexities ensures that the technology continues to evolve in ways that are aligned with human values and beneficial for all.

CHAPTER 4: SHAPING THE FUTURE – AI'S POTENTIAL AND PITFALLS

The Impact of AI on Industry and Society

Artificial Intelligence (AI) is rapidly transforming industries and reshaping society profoundly. As AI technologies advance, they enable automation, optimization, and personalization across various sectors, fundamentally changing the way we live, work, and interact. The implications of AI extend beyond economic productivity, reaching into ethical considerations, social structures, and even global power dynamics.

Revolutionizing Industries

AI's impact is most pronounced in sectors where data-driven decision-making can be leveraged for efficiency and innovation. In healthcare, for example, AI-powered algorithms analyze medical images, predict disease outbreaks, and assist in personalized treatment plans, enhancing patient outcomes and reducing the burden on healthcare systems. Machine learning models can detect patterns in vast datasets, identifying potential health risks earlier than traditional methods.

The manufacturing industry is experiencing a significant transformation with AI-driven automation. Robots and smart machines, guided by AI algorithms, perform repetitive tasks with precision, reducing production costs and increasing output. This shift is leading to a new era of "smart factories," where equipment self-monitors for maintenance needs and supply chains are optimized in real-time.

In finance, AI enhances risk management, fraud detection, and customer service through chatbots and automated trading systems. It allows institutions to analyze market trends and customer behaviors to tailor financial products more effectively. AI's role in the retail sector is similarly influential, with predictive analytics used to optimize inventory, personalize shopping experiences, and recommend products based on consumer preferences.

Transportation is another field where AI is making waves, from autonomous vehicles to predictive maintenance in logistics. Self-driving cars have the potential to reduce traffic accidents and congestion while increasing mobility for people who cannot drive. AI also powers smart traffic management systems that adjust signals based on real-time conditions, leading to more efficient urban mobility.

Societal Impacts

While AI's industrial benefits are clear, its effects on society are more complex. One of the main worries is the displacement of employment due to automation. As machines take over routine tasks, millions of workers may find their skills obsolete, leading to economic disparities and necessitating a shift towards reskilling and upskilling programs. Governments and educational institutions face the challenge of preparing the workforce for an AI-driven economy, emphasizing the need for skills in data science, programming, and other tech-related fields.

AI also raises ethical questions about privacy, surveillance, and decision-making. Facial recognition technology, for example, can enhance security and pose personal privacy risks. The widespread use of AI in decision-making—whether in hiring, law enforcement, or loan approvals—raises concerns about algorithmic bias, as flawed datasets can lead to unfair or discriminatory outcomes.

Another societal implication is the potential deepening of the digital divide. While AI offers opportunities for economic growth, its benefits may not be equitably distributed, with wealthier nations and companies reaping the most advantages. Ensuring that AI advancements benefit society requires policies promoting inclusive development and access to AI education and resources.

AI's impact on industry and society is both transformative and disruptive. It offers unparalleled opportunities for innovation, efficiency, and challenges that require careful management. As AI advances, striking a balance between harnessing its potential and addressing its risks will be essential to ensuring that it serves as a force for good in society.

Addressing Ethical Dilemmas and Regulation Challenges

The rapid advancement of Artificial Intelligence (AI) has introduced profound ethical dilemmas and regulatory challenges. As AI becomes more pervasive, the urgency to address issues around privacy, fairness, transparency, accountability, and societal impact grows. Navigating these dilemmas requires a concerted effort from technologists, policymakers, and ethicists to establish frameworks that ensure AI development aligns with human values and societal well-being.

Ethical Dilemmas in AI Development

Bias and Fairness

One of the most pressing ethical dilemmas in AI is algorithmic bias. When AI models are trained on biased datasets, they can perpetuate and amplify existing inequalities, leading to unfair outcomes in hiring, law enforcement, healthcare, and lending. For instance, facial recognition technology has been found to be less accurate in identifying individuals with darker skin tones, leading to concerns about racial bias. Similarly, AI-based hiring algorithms can unintentionally favor certain demographic groups over others based on historical hiring data that may not reflect equitable practices.

Addressing these issues involves:

Mitigating Bias in Training Data: Developers must ensure that training datasets are diverse, representative, and carefully curated to reduce biases. Techniques like re-weighting data or implementing adversarial training can help achieve more balanced outcomes.

Fairness-Aware Algorithms: Researchers are developing algorithms specifically designed to promote fairness. These algorithms incorporate fairness constraints during training, making it possible to produce models that account for demographic differences and reduce disparities.

Human Oversight: Even with advanced algorithms, human oversight remains crucial. Decision-making processes involving AI should include checks and balances to ensure humans can intervene when biased outcomes occur.

Privacy Concerns

AI's ability to process vast amounts of data raises significant privacy concerns. From facial recognition systems used in public surveillance to recommendation engines that track user behavior, AI applications often involve collecting and analyzing personal data. The challenge is balancing leveraging data to improve AI systems and respecting individuals' privacy rights.

Strategies to address privacy issues include:

Data Anonymization: Data used to train AI models can be anonymized to remove personally identifiable information, although this process may still pose re-identification risks.

Privacy-Preserving Techniques: Methods such as federated learning, which trains models on decentralized data without sharing individual data points, and differential privacy, which adds noise to datasets to mask individual contributions, can enhance privacy protections.

Regulatory Compliance: AI developers must adhere to data protection regulations, such as the General Data Protection Regulation (GDPR) in Europe or the California Consumer Privacy Act (CCPA), which mandate user consent and data minimization practices.

Autonomy and Control

AI systems, particularly those with decision-making capabilities, present challenges regarding autonomy and human control. There is a risk that autonomous AI systems, such as self-driving cars or automated diagnostic tools, could make decisions that are difficult for humans to understand or override. Ensuring that humans remain in control, especially in critical scenarios where AI decisions affect health, safety, or fundamental rights, is a key ethical concern.

Measures to ensure human-centered AI development include:

Human-in-the-Loop Systems: Incorporating human oversight into AI decision-making processes can help maintain control. For instance, in medical diagnostics, AI can assist in suggesting diagnoses, but a human doctor should make the final decision.

Explainability and Transparency: AI systems should be designed to be interpretable so that users can understand how decisions are made. This is particularly important in high-stakes areas like finance, where AI-based credit scoring needs to be transparent to ensure fairness.

Regulatory Challenges in AI Development

Establishing AI Governance Frameworks

The pace of AI development often outstrips the creation of regulatory frameworks, leading to gaps in oversight. Comprehensive AI governance that addresses ethical, safety, and economic impacts without stifling innovation is needed.

Challenges in establishing AI governance include:

Dynamic Nature of AI Technology: As AI rapidly evolves, regulations can quickly become outdated. Flexible, adaptive regulatory frameworks are needed to accommodate emerging technologies and new AI capabilities.

Balancing Innovation and Regulation: Over-regulation can hinder AI development, while under-regulation may leave society vulnerable to the risks associated with AI misuse. Striking the right balance is crucial for promoting responsible AI deployment.

Global Coordination: Since AI development is a worldwide endeavor, international cooperation is needed to set standards and guidelines to prevent regulatory arbitrage, where companies exploit differing regulations across countries.

Ensuring Accountability and Liability

As AI systems take on more decision-making roles, questions arise about accountability and liability when things go wrong. For example, if an autonomous vehicle causes an accident, it is not always clear who is at fault: the manufacturer, the software developer, or the owner of the vehicle. Similarly, if an AI-based medical diagnosis leads to incorrect treatment, determining liability can be challenging.

Approaches to address accountability include:

Clear Liability Rules: Legal frameworks need to be established that define the responsibilities of various stakeholders, including developers, manufacturers, and users, in the deployment of AI systems.

Ethical AI Guidelines: Companies can adopt ethical AI guidelines that set standards for responsible AI use and outline procedures for mitigating risks. Such guidelines can also include auditing mechanisms to ensure compliance with ethical principles.

Insurance and Risk Management: Creating specialized insurance products that cover AI-related risks can help manage liability issues, ensuring that affected parties are compensated in cases where AI systems cause harm.

Addressing the Risks of Autonomous Weapons and AI Militarization

The development of AI-powered weapons and their potential use in military operations poses significant regulatory challenges. Autonomous weapons systems, capable of making life-and-death decisions without human intervention, raise moral and ethical concerns about the loss of human control in warfare.

Regulatory efforts to mitigate these risks involve:

Banning Lethal Autonomous Weapons: Some organizations and policymakers advocate for an outright ban on fully autonomous weapons that can select and engage targets without human oversight. International agreements could be modeled after existing treaties on chemical and nuclear weapons.

Setting Rules of Engagement: Even if autonomous weapons are not banned, it is essential to establish rules of engagement that mandate human oversight and accountability in deploying AI-powered military systems.

Promoting Peaceful AI Development: AI research should prioritize civilian applications that enhance social welfare and economic development, with safeguards against the diversion of technology for military purposes.

Addressing ethical dilemmas and regulatory challenges in AI development is a multi-dimensional effort that requires collaboration across sectors and disciplines. As AI continues to shape industries and society, ethical considerations around fairness, privacy, autonomy, and accountability must be integrated into the development process. Moreover, effective regulatory frameworks are needed to ensure that AI is deployed responsibly and for the benefit of humanity. By proactively addressing these issues, society can harness the transformative power of AI while safeguarding against its potential risks.

Partnerships, Investments, and Strategic Decisions

In the world of technology, partnerships, investments, and strategic decision-making play a crucial role in shaping the trajectory of companies and advancing innovations. Sam Altman has demonstrated a keen understanding of these dynamics through his involvement with various startups, venture capital initiatives, and transformative tech projects. His ability to form strategic partnerships, make calculated investments, and drive pivotal decisions has significantly influenced the tech landscape, especially in areas like AI development and startup growth.

Strategic Partnerships for Growth

One of Altman's notable strengths has been forging partnerships that complement the strengths and goals of the companies he leads. In his role at OpenAI, strategic alliances have been essential in accelerating AI research and broadening the organization's impact. A prime example is the partnership between OpenAI and Microsoft, established in 2019. This collaboration involved a $1 billion investment from Microsoft, aimed at developing artificial general intelligence (AGI) and integrating OpenAI's advanced AI technologies into Microsoft's cloud computing platform, Azure. This partnership enabled OpenAI to leverage Microsoft's massive computing resources to train large AI models and provided Microsoft with cutting-edge AI capabilities, enhancing its position in the cloud market.

Additionally, partnerships with other research institutions and tech companies have allowed for the sharing of knowledge, resources, and best practices. These collaborations help address AI's ethical and technical challenges by pooling expertise from diverse fields, accelerating progress while ensuring that safety and alignment remain priorities.

Investments in AI and Beyond

As an investor, Altman has been strategic in backing companies that demonstrate high potential for innovation and impact. His focus is not limited to AI; he has invested in various technology sectors, from biotech to space exploration. His approach to investment reflects a long-term vision of supporting projects that push the boundaries of what technology can achieve and have the potential to change the world.

Through Y Combinator, Altman played a vital role in funding and nurturing early-stage startups, providing them with the capital, mentorship, and network needed to grow. Startups like Airbnb, Dropbox, and Reddit, which went through Y Combinator, have become industry giants, illustrating the profound impact that early investment and strategic guidance can have on a company's success.

Altman's investment philosophy often involves betting on audacious projects with high risks but potentially transformative outcomes. For example, his investment in companies like SpaceX and Neuralink aligns with his interest in pushing the frontiers of technology, while investments in AI-focused startups demonstrate his commitment to advancing AI responsibly.

Strategic Decisions in AI Development

Strategic decisions at OpenAI have centered around balancing openness with safety in AI development. Initially, OpenAI embraced a philosophy of openness, sharing its research and tools widely to foster collaboration. However, as AI models became more advanced and capable, the risks associated with their misuse grew. This led to a shift in strategy, where OpenAI adopted a more cautious approach to sharing research findings and limited access to powerful AI models like GPT-3 and GPT-4.

This shift was a strategic decision aimed at preventing malicious use of AI while still advancing the field. It demonstrated Altman's commitment to responsible AI development and underscored the complexities of navigating between innovation and safety. By strategically deciding when and how to release AI technologies, OpenAI has managed to maintain a balance between contributing to the research community and safeguarding against potential harm.

Expanding AI's Reach Through Investments

Altman's strategic investments have extended to funding research initiatives and startups that tackle AI's ethical and safety challenges. OpenAI's decision to establish a capped-profit model—allowing for investor returns while prioritizing its mission of benefiting humanity—attracted funding that supports long-term research objectives. This innovative funding approach aligns investors' interests with OpenAI's ethical goals, ensuring that strategic decisions are made with broader societal impact in mind.

Through partnerships, strategic investments, and pivotal decisions, Sam Altman has significantly influenced the development of emerging technologies. His approach demonstrates the importance of leveraging alliances, supporting innovation through investment, and making difficult decisions that balance progress with safety. These elements collectively drive not just the growth of companies but the responsible advancement of technology itself, ensuring that its benefits are maximized while its risks are minimized.

The Role of AI in Global Innovation

Artificial Intelligence (AI) is a driving force behind a new era of global innovation, reshaping industries, accelerating technological development, and addressing some of the world's most pressing challenges. AI's ability to process vast amounts of data, recognize patterns, and make predictions has unlocked unprecedented opportunities across various fields. As a key player in this transformative landscape, AI is not just a tool but a catalyst for innovation, driving progress in science, industry, healthcare, and sustainability on a global scale.

Transforming Industries

AI has become a cornerstone for industry innovation, enabling companies to optimize processes, enhance productivity, and reduce costs. In manufacturing, AI-driven automation allows for precision control of production lines, predictive maintenance of machinery, and efficient supply chain management. This has led to the rise of smart factories, where AI systems make real-time adjustments to improve efficiency and reduce downtime.

The financial sector is also benefiting significantly from AI advancements. Automated trading algorithms, fraud detection systems, and AI-driven customer service solutions such as chatbots have revolutionized the way financial services are delivered. AI is helping institutions assess risks more accurately, detect suspicious activities, and personalize financial products for customers.

In retail, AI is transforming the customer experience through predictive analytics that optimize inventory management, recommendation systems that personalize shopping experiences, and chatbots that provide instant customer support. These applications enable businesses to better understand consumer behavior, respond to market trends, and increase sales.

Driving Scientific Discovery

AI is not only transforming industries but also accelerating scientific research and discovery. In healthcare, AI is used to analyze medical images, predict disease progression, and assist in drug discovery, thereby speeding up the development of new treatments. Machine learning models can identify potential drug candidates by analyzing large datasets of chemical compounds, significantly reducing the time and cost involved in pharmaceutical research.

In the field of physics and astronomy, AI algorithms help process and interpret data from telescopes, identify patterns in cosmic events, and even assist in the search for extraterrestrial life. These advancements allow scientists to make sense of vast amounts of data that would be impossible for humans to analyze manually.

AI is also making strides in climate science by modeling complex environmental systems, predicting weather patterns, and optimizing energy use in smart grids. AI-driven innovations in renewable energy, such as optimizing wind and solar power generation, contribute to global efforts to combat climate change.

Empowering Emerging Economies

One of the most impactful aspects of AI is its potential to empower emerging economies. By providing new tools for economic development, AI can help close the gap between developed and developing countries. In agriculture, AI-driven technologies are used to monitor crop health, predict pest outbreaks, and optimize irrigation, enabling farmers to improve yields and reduce waste. This is particularly valuable in regions where agriculture is a key economic activity and where food security is a concern.

AI is also fostering financial inclusion by enabling the development of fintech solutions that reach underserved populations. For instance, AI-driven credit scoring systems can help extend loans to individuals who lack traditional credit histories, thereby opening up new opportunities for entrepreneurship and economic growth.

Addressing Global Challenges

AI's role in global innovation extends to tackling major global challenges such as climate change, public health, and social inequality. By providing insights through data analysis, AI helps governments and organizations make informed decisions on issues ranging from resource allocation to disaster response. For example, AI-powered early warning systems can predict natural disasters like earthquakes and hurricanes, allowing for better preparedness and potentially saving lives.

In the fight against pandemics, AI has proven valuable in tracking the spread of diseases, modeling infection rates, and even assisting in the development of vaccines. The rapid development of COVID-19 vaccines was partly due to AI's ability to analyze genetic data and accelerate research.

Challenges and Considerations

Despite its transformative potential, the role of AI in global innovation also raises challenges that need to be addressed. Issues such as data privacy, algorithmic bias, and the digital divide can hinder the equitable distribution of AI's benefits. Developing robust regulatory frameworks and promoting ethical AI development are essential to ensure that AI contributes positively to global progress without exacerbating social inequalities.

AI is a powerful driver of global innovation, reshaping industries, accelerating scientific discovery, empowering emerging economies, and addressing some of the most significant global challenges. Its ability to transform data into actionable insights has far-reaching implications for economic growth, scientific research, and social development. However, the ethical and regulatory considerations surrounding AI's deployment must be carefully managed to ensure that its benefits are shared broadly and responsibly. As AI continues to evolve, its role in global innovation will only grow, making it a critical factor in shaping the future of technology and society.

CHAPTER 5: BEYOND TECHNOLOGY – SAM ALTMAN'S BROADER INFLUENCE

Thought Leadership in Tech and Beyond

Thought leadership plays a crucial role in shaping the direction of industries and influencing societal trends, particularly in the technology sector. Thought leaders are more than just experts; they are visionaries who anticipate future trends, advocate for innovative ideas, and inspire others to think differently. In tech, individuals like Sam Altman have leveraged their platforms not only to drive technological advancements but also to shape discussions on ethics, policy, and the broader implications of innovation. Altman's approach to thought leadership extends beyond tech, touching on education, entrepreneurship, and the future of work, making him an influential figure both within and outside the technology community.

Setting the Agenda in AI and Technology

In the rapidly evolving field of AI, thought leadership is essential for guiding responsible development and addressing complex ethical considerations. Altman has used his position to shape discussions about the opportunities and risks associated with AI. As the CEO of OpenAI, he has been a vocal advocate for the responsible use of artificial intelligence, emphasizing the need to balance innovation with safety. His perspective on AI safety is not just about preventing potential misuse but also about ensuring that AI's benefits are distributed equitably across society. By actively participating in discussions on AI ethics, Altman helps shape policies and best practices that influence how AI technologies are developed and deployed.

He has also pushed for more transparency in AI development while recognizing the need for some level of caution. This dual stance—promoting openness in research while limiting access to potentially dangerous AI models—illustrates his thoughtful approach to navigating the complexities of technology leadership. By setting an agenda that balances openness with security, he has contributed to establishing norms that others in the industry follow, thereby shaping the trajectory of AI development globally.

Influencing Entrepreneurship and Startup Culture

Altman's thought leadership extends to entrepreneurship, where he has significantly impacted the startup ecosystem. As a former president of Y Combinator, one of the world's most prominent startup accelerators, he has mentored countless entrepreneurs, helping them scale their businesses and navigate the challenges of early-stage growth. He advocates for bold thinking and taking risks, encouraging startups to tackle big problems rather than focusing solely on incremental improvements.

His insights into startup culture and growth strategies are highly regarded, and his writings and talks on entrepreneurship have become go-to resources for aspiring founders. Altman has emphasized the importance of resilience, adaptability, and long-term vision in building successful companies. By fostering a culture of innovation, he has helped shape the aspirations and strategies of a new generation of entrepreneurs, driving forward a global movement toward tech-driven solutions to real-world problems.

Thought Leadership Beyond Technology

Altman's influence reaches beyond technology into areas like education, universal basic income (UBI), and the future of work. He has expressed support for UBI as a potential solution to the economic displacement caused by automation, proposing that society needs to rethink traditional economic models to adapt to a world where AI and robots perform more tasks previously done by humans. His advocacy for UBI highlights his interest in creating a safety net for individuals in a rapidly changing world, addressing social and economic inequalities exacerbated by technological progress.

He supports reimagining how people learn and prepare for the future in education, advocating for new models that focus on practical skills and lifelong learning rather than traditional credentialing. His forward-thinking views on the future of work challenge conventional assumptions about career trajectories, encouraging people to pursue multiple roles throughout their lives and to continuously adapt to new opportunities.

Inspiring Ethical and Policy Discourse

By taking a proactive stance on the ethical and policy implications of technology, Altman has positioned himself as a leader in advocating for thoughtful regulation and governance of emerging technologies. He frequently engages with policymakers, providing insights into how governments can support innovation while mitigating risks. This engagement is crucial for bridging the gap between rapid technological advances and slow-moving regulatory frameworks.

Altman has also used his platform to discuss the societal responsibilities of tech leaders, urging his peers to consider the broader impact of their innovations. His thought leadership encourages a culture of ethics and accountability within the tech industry, promoting values that go beyond profit-making to include social good.

Sam Altman's thought leadership in tech and beyond demonstrates the power of visionary thinking to influence not just industries, but societal attitudes and policies. By setting the agenda in AI, guiding entrepreneurs, and advocating for innovative solutions to economic and social challenges, he has shaped conversations that extend far beyond technology. His holistic approach to thought leadership—emphasizing ethics, policy, and societal impact—positions him as a key voice in guiding the future direction of both the tech industry and broader societal development.

Philanthropy, Policy, and Public Discourse

Philanthropy, policy, and public discourse are integral aspects of shaping a society where technology serves the common good. Thought leaders like Sam Altman have expanded their influence beyond the boundaries of the technology industry by engaging in these areas, using their resources and platforms to advocate for social change, shape policies, and drive meaningful conversations about the future. Altman's approach to philanthropy, his involvement in policy discussions, and his contributions to public discourse demonstrate a commitment to ensuring that technological advancements benefit all of humanity, not just a privileged few.

Philanthropy for a Tech-Driven Society

Altman's philanthropic efforts focus on addressing some of the societal challenges posed by technological disruption. He recognizes that while technology, especially AI, brings many benefits, it can also contribute to economic inequality, displace jobs, and exacerbate social divides. To counter these effects, his philanthropic endeavors aim to create a more equitable and inclusive future.

One of the major areas where Altman has focused his philanthropic attention is in funding basic research and innovative projects aimed at solving large-scale problems. He has supported organizations and initiatives that work on issues like sustainable energy, education reform, and public health. For instance, investments in sustainable technologies and climate change initiatives reflect his interest in promoting long-term environmental sustainability, a key challenge in the face of global warming and resource scarcity.

Altman has also shown interest in ideas like universal basic income (UBI) as a potential solution to economic displacement caused by automation. He contributed to funding UBI pilot programs, exploring how providing a guaranteed income to individuals could alleviate poverty and empower people to pursue education, entrepreneurship, or other meaningful activities. These pilot programs aim to gather data on UBI's effectiveness in improving economic well-being and inform policymakers on whether it could be a viable solution in the future.

Shaping Policy for Ethical Technology Use

As AI and other technologies become more pervasive, policy discussions about their ethical use, safety, and impact on society are critical. Altman has engaged actively in these conversations, advocating for thoughtful regulation that encourages innovation while protecting individuals' rights and safety. His policy advocacy often revolves around setting guidelines for responsible AI development, emphasizing transparency, fairness, and the prevention of harmful uses.

He has been vocal about the need for a balanced approach to AI regulation, where governments, companies, and researchers collaborate to establish ethical frameworks. For example, Altman supports the idea of government oversight on AI safety to address the risks associated with advanced AI systems, such as autonomous weapons, privacy concerns, and algorithmic bias. His involvement in these policy discussions helps bridge the gap between technologists and lawmakers, ensuring that policies reflect an understanding of both the technological landscape and social implications.

Altman has also contributed to policy discourse around economic and educational reform. He often discusses the future of work in a tech-driven economy, advocating for policies that prepare the workforce for changes brought by automation and AI. This includes promoting lifelong learning programs, skills training, and modernizing education to prioritize practical and adaptable skills over traditional credentialing.

Contributing to Public Discourse

Beyond philanthropy and policy advocacy, Altman has played a key role in shaping public discourse on technology and its impact. He regularly shares his thoughts through blogs, social media, and public speaking engagements, where he addresses pressing issues like AI safety, the economic impact of automation, and the role of startups in driving innovation. Through these platforms, he influences how people think about technology, entrepreneurship, and social responsibility.

His writings on AI ethics, for example, have sparked discussions about the need for transparency in AI development and the societal implications of deploying AI in various fields. By highlighting both the opportunities and risks associated with AI, he encourages a more nuanced understanding of the technology. His stance on AI development has often been characterized by a call for caution without stifling innovation, advocating for measures that ensure AI benefits are broadly shared while minimizing risks.

Altman's public discourse also extends to challenging traditional economic models and proposing alternative solutions, such as UBI. His advocacy for UBI is not just about providing financial support but also about rethinking the nature of work and economic value in a world where machines can perform many tasks previously done by humans. By participating in public debates on these topics, he helps to elevate unconventional ideas into the mainstream, prompting policymakers, academics, and the general public to consider new approaches to longstanding economic and social issues.

Influencing a Broader Social Agenda

Altman's engagement in philanthropy, policy, and public discourse positions him as more than a tech leader; he is also a social influencer with a broader agenda for change. His efforts in these areas aim to ensure that technological progress aligns with societal needs and addresses critical challenges. For instance, by supporting research in AI safety and ethics, he helps establish a foundation for AI development that prioritizes humanity's well-being.

In advocating for policies that anticipate the future workforce's needs, he pushes for reforms that can reduce inequality and prepare society for the challenges posed by technological disruption. Furthermore, his philanthropic investments in UBI and other social experiments provide valuable data for informing policy decisions that could shape a more inclusive economic future.

Sam Altman's work in philanthropy, policy, and public discourse demonstrates a commitment to shaping a future where technology serves as a force for good. His philanthropic efforts address the social challenges brought about by technological change, while his involvement in policy advocacy ensures that ethical considerations are embedded in technology development. Through public discourse, he encourages society to reimagine economic and social systems to be more equitable and resilient in the face of rapid technological progress. Together, these efforts underscore his vision for a tech-driven world that is inclusive, ethical, and forward-looking.

Influencing the Next Generation of Leaders

The impact of a leader is often measured not just by their achievements, but by their ability to inspire and shape the next generation. Sam Altman exemplifies this influence through his work in guiding young entrepreneurs, advocating for forward-thinking educational models, and fostering a mindset of ethical responsibility in leadership. His efforts extend beyond his roles at Y Combinator and OpenAI, encompassing a broader commitment to nurturing the leaders of tomorrow who will shape technology, business, and society in significant ways.

Mentorship and Empowerment

One of Altman's most prominent contributions to developing future leaders has been through mentorship. During his time as president of Y Combinator, he mentored hundreds of startup founders, helping them navigate the complexities of entrepreneurship. His guidance often focused on the fundamentals of building and scaling a business: cultivating resilience, adapting to change, and taking bold risks. Many of the companies that emerged from Y Combinator under his leadership, such as Airbnb, Dropbox, and Reddit, have gone on to become industry leaders, demonstrating the profound impact that early-stage mentorship can have on long-term success.

Altman's mentorship style emphasizes empowering individuals to think beyond conventional limits. He encourages aspiring leaders to tackle significant problems rather than pursuing smaller, incremental innovations. This philosophy is rooted in the belief that ambitious goals drive meaningful change and challenge leaders to push the boundaries of what is possible. By instilling this mindset, Altman helps shape leaders who are not only business-oriented but also socially conscious, aiming to solve some of the world's biggest challenges.

Advocating for Lifelong Learning and Adaptive Skills

Altman also recognizes that preparing the next generation of leaders requires an overhaul of traditional educational models. The rapid pace of technological change means that learning must extend beyond formal education, embracing lifelong skills development. He has advocated for new approaches to education that prioritize practical skills, adaptability, and hands-on experiences over traditional degrees. By supporting initiatives that promote coding, entrepreneurship, and problem-solving skills from an early age, he seeks to prepare individuals to thrive in a tech-driven world.

In his public speeches and writings, Altman often emphasizes the importance of lifelong learning, encouraging young leaders to continuously acquire new skills and adapt to changing circumstances. This approach not only prepares them for technological disruption but also instills a growth mindset—a crucial trait for leaders who must navigate uncertainty and drive innovation in an evolving landscape.

Instilling Ethical Leadership and Social Responsibility

Altman's influence extends beyond technical and entrepreneurial skills to encompass ethical leadership. In his discussions about AI, automation, and future work, he has emphasized the responsibility that comes with wielding technological power. He advocates for leaders to consider the broader social and ethical implications of their actions, particularly when it comes to technologies that could impact millions of lives.

By incorporating discussions of ethics and societal impact into conversations about innovation, Altman encourages future leaders to prioritize the well-being of humanity alongside profitability. This approach helps create a generation of leaders who are not only capable of driving technological advancements but are also committed to ensuring those advancements benefit society as a whole. His advocacy for ethical decision-making in the tech industry sets a standard for responsible leadership that others can follow.

Building Communities of Future Innovators

Altman's commitment to influencing the next generation is also evident in his efforts to build and nurture communities of innovators. Y Combinator itself is more than just an accelerator; it is a thriving network where entrepreneurs learn from one another and share experiences. By fostering a collaborative environment, Altman helps create a culture where young leaders support each other's growth, share resources, and work together to solve problems.

Beyond Y Combinator, his work in AI and technology has connected thought leaders across different fields, facilitating dialogues that go beyond the immediate interests of their industries. This interdisciplinary approach encourages young innovators to think holistically and recognize the interconnected nature of technology, society, and the economy.

Sam Altman's efforts in influencing the next generation of leaders encompass mentorship, advocacy for modern education, ethical leadership, and community-building. Through his guidance at Y Combinator, his public advocacy for lifelong learning, and his insistence on the importance of social responsibility, he is shaping a new wave of leaders who are not only equipped to drive technological progress but are also committed to making a positive impact on society. His approach creates a foundation for sustainable leadership in a world that demands continuous adaptation, ethical considerations, and bold innovation.

Personal Philosophy on Work, Life, and Success

Sam Altman's personal philosophy on work, life, and success reflects a blend of ambition, adaptability, and a commitment to making a positive impact on society. His views emphasize the importance of bold thinking, resilience in the face of challenges, continuous learning, and ethical responsibility. As a thought leader and entrepreneur, he advocates for a life driven by purpose rather than just financial gain, emphasizing the significance of pursuing work that is meaningful, while also maintaining a balanced approach to life.

The Value of Ambition and Bold Thinking

A cornerstone of Altman's philosophy is the belief in setting ambitious goals and tackling significant challenges. He often advises aspiring entrepreneurs to think big and aim for transformative impact, rather than settling for incremental improvements. This approach is not just about pursuing the largest possible financial success, but about making a meaningful difference in the world. He encourages taking calculated risks and embracing the possibility of failure, which he sees as a natural part of the learning and growth process. For Altman, aiming high pushes individuals out of their comfort zones, fosters innovation, and leads to personal and professional growth.

Resilience and Adaptability

Altman places a strong emphasis on the importance of resilience. In his view, setbacks and failures are inevitable in the journey toward success, especially in the volatile world of startups and technology. The key is not to avoid failure altogether but to learn from it, adapt quickly, and keep moving forward. He often advises young entrepreneurs to maintain a long-term perspective and not be discouraged by temporary difficulties, advocating for a mindset that sees challenges as opportunities for growth. His own career, which includes ventures that did not always go as planned, exemplifies this resilience and the ability to adapt to new circumstances.

Lifelong Learning and Continuous Improvement

Another vital element of Altman's philosophy is the commitment to lifelong learning and personal development. He believes that the rapid pace of technological change requires individuals to continuously acquire new skills and stay curious. Altman sees learning as a never-ending process that extends beyond formal education, encouraging people to read extensively, experiment, and engage in projects that stretch their capabilities. This approach fosters a growth mindset, where success is not defined by a single accomplishment but by ongoing improvement and adaptation.

Balance Between Work and Life

While Altman is known for his intense focus and work ethic, he also values the importance of maintaining a balance between work and personal life. He recognizes that burnout can be detrimental to long-term success and advocates for a lifestyle that includes time for rest, hobbies, and personal interests. He believes that achieving this balance not only makes life more fulfilling but also enhances productivity and creativity. By prioritizing activities that recharge the mind and body, individuals can sustain high levels of performance over the long term.

Success as a Responsibility

Altman's definition of success goes beyond financial metrics or career achievements; it encompasses ethical responsibility and the impact one's work has on society. He believes that those who achieve success, especially in the tech industry, have a responsibility to consider the broader consequences of their innovations. For instance, his work on AI safety and ethics reflects a commitment to ensuring that technological progress does not come at the expense of societal well-being. He encourages leaders to use their influence to drive positive change and address critical issues, such as economic inequality and environmental sustainability.

Purpose-Driven Work

Central to Altman's philosophy is the idea that work should be purpose-driven. He often speaks about the importance of finding a mission that inspires and motivates, rather than simply working for financial rewards. This sense of purpose fuels passion and determination, making it easier to persevere through difficult times. In his own career, he has focused on projects that he believes have the potential to change the world, such as AI research and startup development. This approach aligns with his broader view that success is not just about personal gain but about contributing to the advancement of society.

Sam Altman's personal philosophy on work, life, and success encompasses ambition, resilience, lifelong learning, balance, ethical responsibility, and purpose-driven action. By encouraging others to think boldly, adapt to challenges, and commit to continuous growth, he promotes a holistic approach to success that goes beyond traditional measures. His belief in the ethical use of technology and the pursuit of meaningful work serves as a guiding principle for those who seek not only to succeed in their careers but also to make a positive impact on the world.

Chapter 6: The Road Ahead – Pioneering New Frontiers

Future Visions for OpenAI and Artificial Intelligence

The future of OpenAI, under Sam Altman's leadership, is shaped by a vision of advancing artificial intelligence (AI) in a way that maximizes its benefits for society while mitigating potential risks. Altman's ambitions for AI are not merely about making technological breakthroughs but about fundamentally improving human life, addressing global challenges, and democratizing access to the benefits of AI. His future vision for OpenAI includes transforming industries, enhancing human capabilities, and ensuring the safe and ethical deployment of AI systems.

Transforming Industries and Solving Global Problems

Altman sees AI as a powerful tool that can revolutionize various industries by increasing efficiency, optimizing processes, and enabling new innovations. Sectors like healthcare, education, finance, and logistics stand to benefit significantly from AI advancements. In healthcare, for example, AI could assist in diagnosing diseases, personalizing treatment plans, and accelerating the development of new drugs. In education, AI-driven personalized learning could help close achievement gaps and provide customized support for students.

Moreover, Altman envisions AI playing a pivotal role in addressing global challenges, such as climate change, food security, and energy sustainability. By applying AI to optimize energy use, improve agricultural practices, and accelerate scientific research, OpenAI aims to tackle some of humanity's most pressing problems. The goal is not only to improve existing systems but to enable breakthroughs that were previously considered out of reach.

Enhancing Human Capabilities

A key aspect of Altman's vision for AI is its ability to enhance human capabilities rather than replace them. He believes AI should serve as a tool that amplifies human potential, making people more productive and creative. For instance, AI can assist professionals by handling repetitive tasks, allowing them to focus on higher-value work that requires complex decision-making, emotional intelligence, and creativity. This augmentation of human capabilities could reshape the nature of work and help people achieve more in their personal and professional lives.

Altman's concept of AI-powered tools extends to everyday use, where AI could be integrated seamlessly into people's lives to help with tasks like scheduling, information retrieval, and communication. By making AI accessible and useful to a broad audience, OpenAI aims to democratize its benefits and reduce the digital divide.

Ensuring Ethical Development and Safety

Altman has consistently emphasized the need for responsible and ethical AI development. His future vision includes a robust framework for AI governance that prioritizes safety, fairness, and transparency. He advocates for regulations and oversight mechanisms that ensure AI technologies do not cause harm, are free from biases, and are used for the public good.

OpenAI's approach to AI development involves both advancing the technology and setting safety standards. Altman supports the idea of collaborative efforts between AI developers, governments, and civil society to create guidelines that balance innovation with risk management. His goal is to make sure that AI's benefits are widely shared and that no single entity has disproportionate control over this powerful technology.

Democratizing AI and Avoiding Concentrated Power

A crucial aspect of Altman's vision for the future of OpenAI is the democratization of AI. He believes AI's power should not be concentrated in the hands of a few large corporations or governments, which could lead to monopolistic control or misuse. Instead, OpenAI is committed to developing AI in a way that spreads its advantages widely, enabling diverse groups to participate in shaping the future of technology.

Sam Altman's vision for the future of OpenAI and artificial intelligence is centered on leveraging AI to solve global challenges, enhance human capabilities, and promote ethical development. By focusing on democratizing access to AI and ensuring its safe deployment, he seeks to create a future where AI benefits are shared broadly, contributing to a more equitable and prosperous world.

Speculating on the Next Big Bets

Sam Altman has always been forward-thinking in identifying and investing in technologies that have the potential to disrupt industries and transform the world. His focus extends beyond traditional tech innovations, venturing into areas that could redefine the way we live, work, and solve pressing global challenges. The "next big bets" that Altman is likely to focus on include advancements in artificial intelligence (AI), climate change solutions, biotechnology, and space exploration. Each of these areas carries significant risks and rewards but promises to push the boundaries of what is currently possible.

AI and General Artificial Intelligence

Artificial intelligence continues to be at the forefront of Altman's big bets, particularly the pursuit of general artificial intelligence (AGI). While current AI models excel at specific tasks, AGI refers to a more advanced form of AI that can understand, learn, and apply knowledge across a wide range of activities, much like a human. Altman sees AGI as one of the most profound technological advancements humanity could achieve, potentially revolutionizing every sector from healthcare to manufacturing. The development of AGI would not only enhance productivity but could also lead to solutions for complex problems that are currently unsolvable, such as finding cures for diseases or addressing large-scale social issues like poverty.

However, Altman is also mindful of the ethical and safety considerations surrounding AGI. Therefore, his approach includes parallel efforts in creating safety frameworks, collaborating on AI governance, and setting industry standards to ensure that AGI development remains beneficial and does not pose existential risks.

Climate Change and Clean Energy Solutions

Another area where Altman sees immense potential is in combating climate change through clean energy innovations and environmental technology. As the world grapples with the effects of global warming, finding sustainable energy solutions is critical. Altman has shown interest in technologies like nuclear fusion, carbon capture, and renewable energy advancements, which could serve as scalable alternatives to fossil fuels. If successful, these technologies could fundamentally alter the energy landscape, reduce carbon emissions, and help mitigate the worst impacts of climate change.

Nuclear fusion, in particular, is seen as a game-changing technology that could provide a nearly limitless and clean energy source. Although it remains in the experimental stages, significant breakthroughs in fusion technology could change the global energy economy and become a multi-trillion-dollar industry. Altman's investments in startups exploring fusion and other clean energy technologies highlight his commitment to addressing environmental issues while capitalizing on emerging markets.

Biotechnology and Longevity

Biotechnology, especially in the realm of health and longevity, is another area poised for disruptive breakthroughs. Altman believes that extending human lifespan and improving quality of life through genetic engineering, personalized medicine, and anti-aging therapies will be a focal point of the next wave of innovation. Advances in CRISPR gene-editing technology, regenerative medicine, and early disease detection could transform healthcare from a reactive system to a preventive one.

The potential for biotech to drastically improve human health also aligns with his interest in leveraging technology to solve significant social problems. Investments in longevity startups or companies focused on eradicating age-related diseases are likely areas where Altman will place big bets.

Space Exploration and the Final Frontier

Space exploration is another exciting area where Altman sees potential. As the cost of launching and operating space missions continues to decrease, he believes that space technology will become a more viable sector for innovation. This includes satellite technology, asteroid mining, and even colonization of other planets. Investing in companies that aim to develop infrastructure for space travel could open up new economic opportunities and provide solutions for resource scarcity on Earth.

Sam Altman's speculated next big bets span across AI, climate solutions, biotechnology, and space exploration. Each represents a frontier where technological advancements could profoundly shape the future, addressing some of humanity's greatest challenges while also presenting high-risk, high-reward opportunities. By focusing on these sectors, Altman aims to not only push the boundaries of technological progress but also solve problems that could benefit society as a whole.

Challenges and Opportunities in a Rapidly Changing World

The 21st century is defined by rapid technological advances, shifting economic landscapes, and evolving societal expectations, creating both challenges and opportunities. Leaders like Sam Altman navigate this fast-paced environment by leveraging innovation to solve problems while addressing potential risks. Understanding these challenges and opportunities is crucial for maximizing the benefits of change while minimizing its downsides. The most significant areas of focus include technological disruption, economic inequality, climate change, and ethical considerations in innovation.

Technological Disruption and Workforce Shifts

One of the major challenges of a rapidly changing world is the displacement of traditional jobs due to technological advancements. Automation, artificial intelligence (AI), and robotics are transforming industries, leading to fears of job losses and economic disruption. Workers in manufacturing, retail, and even some white-collar professions face uncertainty as machines and software increasingly take on tasks once performed by humans. This creates a societal challenge: how to balance technological progress with the need to provide meaningful employment and economic stability.

At the same time, these technological shifts present significant opportunities. They enable increased productivity, cost reduction, and the creation of entirely new industries. The development of AI, for example, not only automates tasks but also opens doors to advancements in healthcare, logistics, and data analysis. Embracing these technologies could lead to a more efficient economy and potentially create new types of jobs that we cannot yet foresee. The challenge lies in preparing the workforce for these changes through reskilling, education, and policies that promote job creation in emerging sectors.

Economic Inequality and Access to Opportunities

The wealth gap and economic inequality are exacerbated by rapid technological change, as the benefits of innovation are not always evenly distributed. Those with access to technology and the skills to leverage it stand to gain the most, while others may be left behind. This disparity can lead to social unrest and hinder economic growth by limiting opportunities for large segments of the population. Addressing these inequalities requires proactive measures to ensure access to technology, quality education, and fair economic policies.

However, the fast-paced evolution of technology also provides an opportunity to reduce inequality. Innovations in online education, for instance, democratize access to learning, allowing people from all backgrounds to gain valuable skills. Similarly, digital platforms can connect entrepreneurs in developing regions to global markets, creating new economic opportunities. By ensuring that technology is used to bridge gaps rather than widen them, society can leverage innovation to foster a more inclusive economy.

Climate Change and Environmental Sustainability

Climate change poses a significant challenge in a rapidly changing world, as industrial growth and technological advancements have come at the cost of environmental degradation. The urgent need to reduce carbon emissions, manage natural resources sustainably, and address the impact of global warming demands innovative solutions.

The shift towards sustainable energy sources, such as solar and wind, represents an opportunity to combat climate change while creating new industries. Additionally, breakthroughs in fields like nuclear fusion, carbon capture, and green technology offer hope for a sustainable future. Companies and governments are increasingly investing in environmental tech, recognizing the potential for economic growth through sustainable practices. The challenge is to accelerate the adoption of these solutions while balancing economic development with ecological preservation.

Ethical Considerations and Regulation

Rapid technological advancements also raise ethical concerns about privacy, security, and the responsible use of innovations like AI and genetic engineering. These developments often outpace existing regulatory frameworks, creating a dilemma on how to govern new technologies effectively without stifling innovation. The challenge is to implement regulations that protect societal interests while allowing room for growth and experimentation.

At the same time, this period of rapid change provides an opportunity to set new ethical standards. By fostering transparent, inclusive dialogue about the implications of new technologies, society can shape a future where technological progress aligns with human values.

The challenges and opportunities of a rapidly changing world are intertwined, creating a complex landscape where technological disruption, economic inequality, climate change, and ethical considerations must be addressed. By embracing innovation, fostering inclusive growth, and prioritizing sustainability, leaders can navigate these challenges and harness opportunities to build a more equitable and prosperous future.

What's Next for Sam Altman

As one of the most influential figures in technology and innovation, Sam Altman is likely to continue playing a pivotal role in shaping the future of artificial intelligence (AI), climate solutions, and other frontier technologies. With a track record of leading transformative initiatives, his next steps will involve deepening his focus on high-impact areas, tackling global challenges, and driving innovation across multiple industries. While much remains speculative, several key areas are likely to define Altman's future trajectory, including advancements in AI, tackling climate change, exploring biotechnology, and perhaps venturing further into policy and thought leadership.

Continuing AI Advancement at OpenAI

Altman's ongoing work at OpenAI suggests that AI will remain central to his future plans. As AI technology evolves, he is expected to push the boundaries further towards achieving general artificial intelligence (AGI), which could have profound implications across sectors. His focus will likely include enhancing the capabilities of AI models, making them more human-like in understanding and problem-solving, while addressing the ethical and safety challenges that come with more powerful AI systems.

Given the growing regulatory interest in AI, Altman may also play a significant role in shaping AI governance. He has already participated in discussions around AI safety and ethics, advocating for a balanced approach to regulation that ensures both innovation and protection. As AI becomes even more integrated into daily life, Altman is likely to work closely with policymakers to establish global standards that guide AI development responsibly.

Tackling Climate Change and Clean Energy

In addition to AI, climate change is another area where Altman has demonstrated interest and potential for impact. With his investments in nuclear fusion startups and other clean energy technologies, Altman aims to be part of the solution to one of the world's most pressing problems. He sees clean energy, particularly nuclear fusion, as a transformative technology that could provide a nearly limitless supply of sustainable power.

Over the next few years, we can expect Altman to increase his involvement in clean energy projects, helping to accelerate the commercialization of technologies that can significantly reduce carbon emissions. This may also include expanding investments in carbon capture, renewable energy innovations, and energy storage solutions, aiming to make a tangible difference in combating climate change.

Biotechnology and Health Innovations

Biotechnology, especially in the areas of health, longevity, and personalized medicine, is another field where Altman might place his focus. As advancements in genetic engineering, regenerative medicine, and artificial intelligence converge, there is immense potential to revolutionize healthcare by predicting, preventing, and curing diseases more effectively.

Altman may support startups and research efforts aimed at extending human lifespan, improving the quality of life, and using data-driven approaches to health. This aligns with his broader goal of solving big problems that have a direct impact on humanity, and biotechnology represents a frontier with untapped possibilities.

Thought Leadership and Policy Influence

Beyond technology development, Altman's future may include more active roles in policy and thought leadership. His views on technology's impact on society, ethical AI development, and the future of work position him as a key voice in shaping public discourse. Altman could engage more deeply with global leaders and institutions, advocating for responsible innovation while driving technological progress.

New Entrepreneurial Ventures

Given Altman's history as a serial entrepreneur, there is also the possibility that he will embark on new ventures, exploring opportunities in fields like space exploration, digital currencies, or other emerging technologies. His interest in "moonshot" projects that seek to solve large-scale problems could lead him to take on ambitious initiatives that stretch beyond his current focus areas.

The next chapter for Sam Altman is likely to be defined by continued innovation in AI, expanded efforts to combat climate change, exploration of biotechnology, and increased influence in public policy and thought leadership. His commitment to solving big problems and improving the human condition suggests that his future endeavors will push the boundaries of what's possible, driving forward technological and social progress.

CONCLUSION

The Legacy of a Tech Pioneer

Sam Altman's legacy as a tech pioneer is one of transformative influence across multiple domains, including artificial intelligence, entrepreneurship, and innovation. His work has not only shaped the trajectory of modern technology but has also influenced how society navigates the ethical and practical implications of rapid technological change. Altman's legacy is defined by his leadership at OpenAI, his role in nurturing the startup ecosystem, and his commitment to solving some of humanity's most pressing challenges, such as climate change and inequality.

Pioneering Artificial Intelligence Development

Altman's most significant and enduring legacy is likely to be his impact on artificial intelligence. As CEO of OpenAI, he has overseen the development of some of the world's most advanced AI models, including GPT-3, GPT-4, and GPT-5, which have set new benchmarks in natural language processing and machine learning. His vision extends beyond creating powerful AI models to pursuing the ultimate goal of general artificial intelligence (AGI), an AI system capable of performing any intellectual task that a human can.

Through OpenAI, Altman has emphasized the importance of responsible AI development, advocating for ethical standards, safety protocols, and collaboration between industry and government to manage AI's risks. His approach has helped shape the public conversation around AI, steering it toward a balance between innovation and caution. If AGI is realized, Altman's role in guiding its development will be seen as one of the most significant contributions in the history of technology.

Nurturing the Startup Ecosystem

Before his involvement with OpenAI, Altman made a profound impact as the president of Y Combinator, one of the world's most influential startup accelerators. Under his leadership, Y Combinator grew exponentially, funding companies like Airbnb, Dropbox, and Reddit. Altman's approach to mentorship and investment not only fostered a culture of innovation but also provided young entrepreneurs with the resources and guidance needed to succeed in a highly competitive market.

His legacy in the startup world goes beyond individual companies to shaping the culture of Silicon Valley. He advocated for a shift from pursuing growth at all costs to focusing on solving meaningful problems. By championing mission-driven companies and supporting startups addressing societal challenges, Altman helped redefine what success looks like in the tech world, placing value on impact alongside financial returns.

Addressing Global Challenges Through Technology

Altman's legacy will also be marked by his efforts to tackle global challenges like climate change, energy sustainability, and inequality. His investments in clean energy technologies, including nuclear fusion and carbon capture, demonstrate a commitment to leveraging technology for environmental sustainability. He has taken the stance that solving big problems requires bold and sometimes unconventional approaches, and his support for "moonshot" projects reflects this belief.

Furthermore, Altman has spoken about the need to address economic inequality exacerbated by technological advances. By advocating for policies such as universal basic income and equitable access to technology, he has contributed to the broader dialogue about how society can ensure that the benefits of innovation are widely shared.

Ethical Leadership and Shaping the Future of Tech Policy

Altman's influence extends beyond technological innovation to thought leadership and policy. His vocal stance on the ethical development of AI and his push for regulatory frameworks demonstrate a commitment to ensuring technology is used for the public good. He has become a key figure in the conversation about technology's impact on society, advocating for a future where technology aligns with human values.

The legacy of Sam Altman as a tech pioneer is multi-faceted, encompassing his work in AI development, contributions to the startup ecosystem, and efforts to solve global challenges. His vision for technology as a force for good, combined with his influence on the ethical standards guiding its development, will leave a lasting mark on the future of innovation. Altman's enduring legacy will be defined by his drive to push boundaries while fostering a more equitable and sustainable world.

Reflections on Innovation, Leadership, and the Future of Technology

Sam Altman's reflections on innovation, leadership, and the future of technology provide a roadmap for navigating the complex landscape of modern technological advancement. With his experiences as a tech entrepreneur, investor, and CEO of OpenAI, Altman has a unique perspective on the forces shaping the world. His views on these topics are not just theoretical; they are grounded in a commitment to addressing real-world challenges, pushing the boundaries of what's possible, and ensuring that technology serves the greater good.

Innovation as a Force for Good

Altman believes that true innovation should not merely create new products but should solve meaningful problems and improve the quality of life. His work at OpenAI exemplifies this approach, as the company's AI research aims to develop technologies that augment human capabilities, facilitate scientific discoveries, and make processes more efficient. According to Altman, the greatest innovations are those that fundamentally change how society functions, such as breakthroughs in AI, renewable energy, and biotechnology.

However, Altman also recognizes that innovation is a double-edged sword. While it can lead to substantial benefits, it can also disrupt industries and displace workers. Thus, he advocates for a thoughtful approach to innovation, where technological advancements are accompanied by measures to mitigate negative societal impacts, such as retraining programs for workers affected by automation.

Leadership in a Rapidly Changing Technology Landscape

As a leader, Altman emphasizes the importance of adaptability and resilience in a world where change is the only constant. He believes that successful leadership involves not just setting a vision but also being able to pivot when faced with new information or changing circumstances. This adaptability was evident during his tenure at Y Combinator, where he transformed the accelerator into a global force for startup growth, and at OpenAI, where he navigates the challenges of leading cutting-edge AI research while addressing ethical and safety concerns.

Altman often highlights the role of mission-driven leadership. He argues that the best leaders are motivated not only by profit but by a larger purpose that guides their decisions. In the case of OpenAI, the mission is to ensure that artificial intelligence benefits all of humanity. By setting ambitious yet ethical goals, Altman demonstrates that leadership in technology requires balancing aggressive pursuit of innovation with a sense of responsibility.

The Future of Technology: Balancing Potential and Risk

Looking ahead, Altman sees immense potential in emerging technologies, particularly in AI, clean energy, and life sciences. He believes that artificial intelligence will be one of the most transformative technologies of the century, potentially unlocking solutions to complex problems in healthcare, logistics, and climate change. However, this transformation also brings risks, particularly in the areas of privacy, security, and job displacement. Altman advocates for proactive regulation and collaboration between governments, companies, and researchers to establish ethical guidelines and safety protocols.

Altman is also a strong proponent of focusing on "moonshot" projects—high-risk, high-reward ventures that aim to solve major global challenges. His support for initiatives like nuclear fusion as a clean energy source and longevity research reflects his belief that technology should not only improve current systems but redefine them.

The Ethical Imperative

Central to Altman's reflections is the notion that ethical considerations must be embedded in the development of technology from the outset. He stresses that leaders in technology have a moral obligation to think about the long-term consequences of their innovations. This includes not only the intended benefits but also potential misuse or unintended consequences, such as bias in AI algorithms or surveillance risks.

Sam Altman's reflections on innovation, leadership, and the future of technology offer valuable insights into the delicate balance between pushing the boundaries of what is possible and addressing the ethical implications of such advancements. His perspective underscores the need for mission-driven leadership, responsible innovation, and a commitment to leveraging technology for the greater good. As the tech landscape continues to evolve, Altman's approach serves as a guiding light for future leaders aiming to create impactful, sustainable, and ethical advancements.

Printed in Great Britain
by Amazon

bc5f6b3c-9fdf-4313-baf0-6956f44d4dabR01